1974 · A Time Traveler's Guide: Flashback

A Year to Re

1974

For Those Whose Hearts Belong to 1974

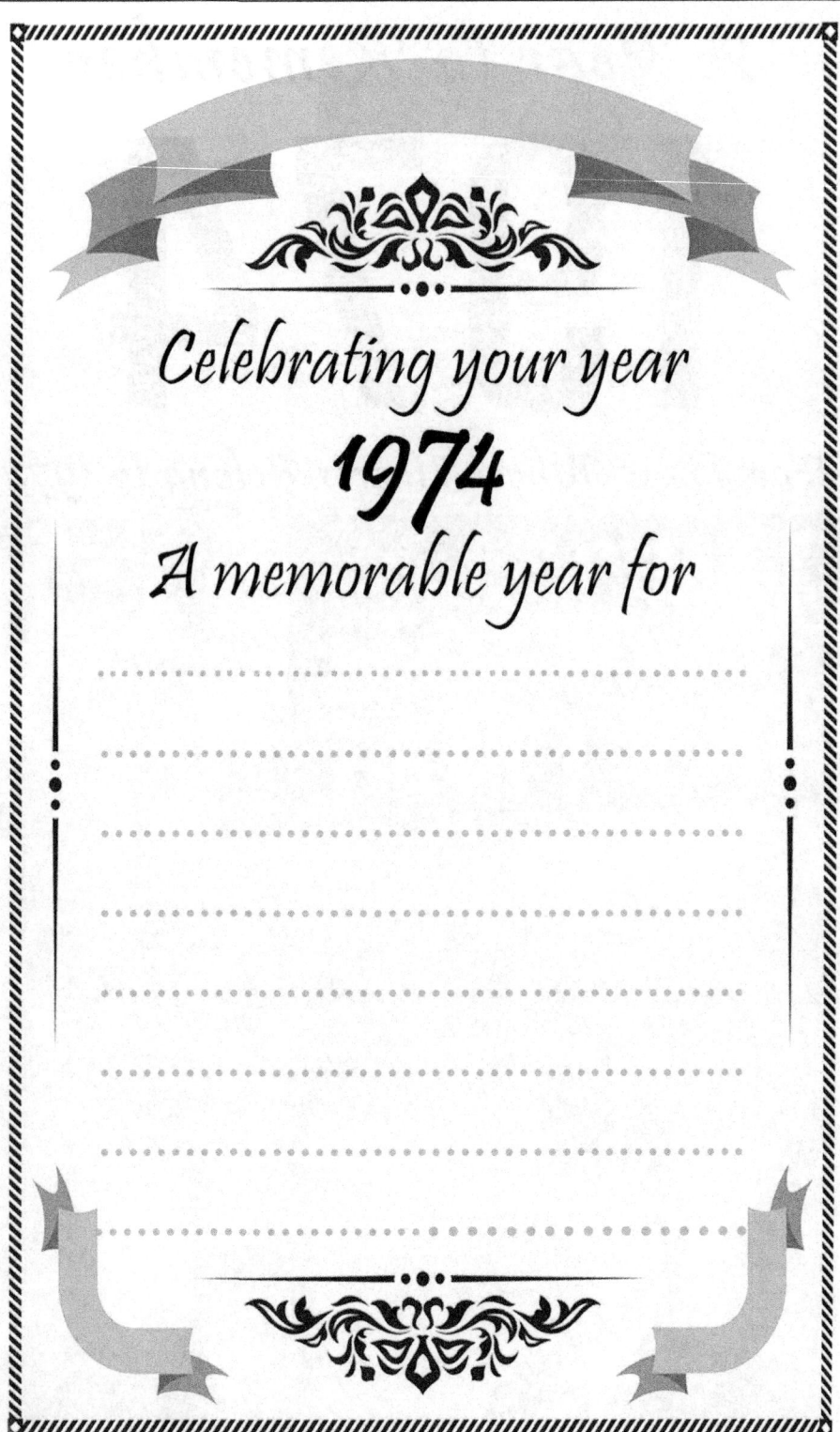

Contents

Introduction: A Glimpse into 1974..................5

Chapter 1: Politics and Leading Events around the World
1.1 The Global Stage in 1974: Where Were You?.........6
1.2 Leaders and Statesmen: Movers and Shakers of '74..................10
Activity: Historical Crossword - Test Your Knowledge of '74..................14

Chapter 2: The Iconic Movies, TV Shows, and Awards
2.1 Memorable Films of '74..................15
2.2 TV Shows That Captivated the Nation..................19
2.3 Prestigious Film Awards and Honors..................21
Activity: Movie and TV Show Trivia Quiz - How Well Do You Know '74 Entertainment?..................23

Chapter 3: Music: Top Songs, Albums, and Awards
3.1 Renowned Musicians and Bands of '74..................24
3.2 Notable Albums and Song Releases..................27
3.3 Music Awards and Honors..................29
Activity: Music Lyrics Challenge - Guess the Song Lyrics from '74..................35

Chapter 4: Sporting highlights in 1974..................40
Activity: Sports Trivia - Test Your Knowledge of 1974 Sports History..................45

Chapter 5: Pop Culture, Fashion, and Popular Leisure Activities
5.1 Fashion Flashback: What the World Wore in '74..........47
5.2 Leisure Pursuits: Entertainment and Hobbies..................54
Activity: Fashion Design Coloring Page - Create Your '74-Inspired Outfit..................57

Chapter 6: Technological Advancements and Popular Cars
6.1 Innovations That Shaped the Future..................60
6.2 The Automobiles of '74..................64
Activity: Classic Car Match-Up - Pair the Cars with Their Names..................69

Chapter 7: Stats and the Cost of Things
7.1 The Cost of Living in 1974..................75
Activity: 1974 Shopping List Challenge..................78

Chapter 8: The Famous Wedding and Divorce of 1974
8.1 Famous weddings..................81
8.2 Famous divorces..................86
Activity: Wedding and Divorce Timeline Challenge..................90

Reflecting on 1974
Relaxing Corner - 1974 Review Crossword..................95
Special gifts for readers..................97
Activity answers..................101

Introduction

A Year to Remember - 1974
For Those Whose Hearts Belong to 1974
To our cherished readers who hold a special connection to the year 1974, whether it's because you were born in this remarkable year, celebrated a milestone, or hold dear memories from that time, this book is a tribute to you and your unique connection to an unforgettable era.

In the pages that follow, we invite you to embark on a captivating journey back to 1974, a year of profound historical significance. For those with a personal connection to this year, it holds a treasure trove of memories, stories, and experiences that shaped the world and touched your lives.

Throughout this book, we've woven together the tapestry of 1974, providing historical insights, personal stories, and interactive activities that allow you to relive and celebrate the significance of this special year.

As you turn the pages and immerse yourself in the events and culture of 1974, we hope you'll find moments of nostalgia, inspiration, and the opportunity to rekindle cherished memories of this extraordinary year.

This book is dedicated to you, our readers, who share a unique bond with 1974. May it bring you joy, enlightenment, and a deeper connection to the rich tapestry of history that weaves through your lives.

With warm regards,
Edward Art Lab

Chapter 1: Politics and Leading Events around the World

1.1 The Global Stage of 1974 in America: Where Were You?

In 1974, the global stage was marked by several significant events, and the United States played a central role in many of them. Here are some key moments that shaped the global stage in America during that year:

Watergate Scandal

The Watergate scandal was a defining moment in American politics. It revolved around the break-in at the Democratic National Committee headquarters in 1972, which was linked to the reelection campaign of President Richard Nixon. By 1974, the scandal had reached its climax. On August 8, 1974, Richard Nixon became the first U.S. president to resign from office, facing impeachment over his involvement in the scandal.

Gerald Ford's Presidency

With Nixon's resignation, Vice President Gerald Ford assumed the presidency, becoming the 38th President of the United States. Ford's presidency was marked by efforts to heal the nation after the Watergate crisis, including his controversial decision to pardon Nixon.

Energy Crisis

In the early 1970s, the United States faced an energy crisis, exacerbated by the OPEC oil embargo, which had begun in 1973. This crisis led to long lines at gas stations, energy conservation measures, and discussions about the country's dependence on foreign oil.

Economy and Inflation

The U.S. economy in 1974 faced challenges such as high inflation and unemployment. These economic issues were a cause for concern and shaped the policy decisions of the Ford administration.

The Fall of Saigon

While not in 1974 itself, the Vietnam War came to an end in April 1975 with the fall of Saigon. The events leading up to this moment in 1974, including the withdrawal of U.S. troops, had a profound impact on American foreign policy and the nation's self-image.

Cultural and Social Movements

In 1974, the United States continued to experience cultural and social shifts, with movements like feminism and civil rights activism making significant strides. The era was marked by debates over issues like women's rights, racial equality, and environmentalism.

1.2 Leaders and Statesmen: Movers and Shakers of '74

The year 1974 saw several influential leaders and statesmen who played pivotal roles on the world stage. Here are some notable figures from that year:

Richard Nixon

Richard Nixon served as the 37th President of the United States until his resignation on August 8, 1974, amid the Watergate scandal.

Leonid Brezhnev

Leonid Brezhnev was the General Secretary of the Communist Party of the Soviet Union in 1974, and he played a crucial role in Cold War politics.

Henry Kissinger

Henry Kissinger was the U.S. Secretary of State under both Nixon and Ford and was a key figure in shaping American foreign policy during this period.

Anwar Sadat

Anwar Sadat served as the President of Egypt in 1974 and later played a significant role in peace negotiations with Israel, culminating in the Camp David Accords in 1978.

Golda Meir

Golda Meir was the Prime Minister of Israel in 1974, leading the country during a period of regional tension and conflict.

Nelson Mandela

Nelson Mandela, although imprisoned in 1974, continued to be a symbol of resistance against apartheid in South Africa, a struggle that gained increasing international attention. These leaders and statesmen left an indelible mark on the political landscape of 1974, influencing both national and international affairs.

Queen Elizabeth II's Triumph at the 1974 Commonwealth Games in Christchurch, New Zealand

In February 1974, Queen Elizabeth II graced the Commonwealth Games with her presence in Christchurch, New Zealand. This historic occasion marked a significant moment not only in the world of sports but also in the enduring relationship between the British monarchy and the Commonwealth nations.

Amidst the vibrant atmosphere of the Commonwealth Games, Queen Elizabeth II took on the role of presenting medals to the victorious athletes. With grace and regal dignity, she bestowed the medals upon the deserving winners, symbolizing the spirit of fair competition, sportsmanship, and camaraderie that the Commonwealth Games represent.

The Grand Gathering: Order of the British Empire Service at St. Paul's Cathedral, 1974

On the 23rd of May 1974, a prestigious and ceremonial event took place at St. Paul's Cathedral in London, England. Queen Elizabeth II and Prince Philip, the Duke of Edinburgh, graced the occasion with their regal presence. They arrived at the cathedral to attend the Order of the British Empire (OBE) Service.

The OBE is one of the highest honors in the United Kingdom, recognizing outstanding contributions and achievements in various fields, including public service, arts, sciences, and more. The service at St. Paul's Cathedral was a solemn and dignified gathering where recipients of the OBE and members of the Order came together to celebrate their accomplishments and reaffirm their commitment to the principles of the order.

1974   A Time Traveler's Guide: Flashback Series of Memorial Books   16

Chapter 2: The Iconic Movies, TV Shows, nd Awards

2.1 Hollywood's Finest: Memorable Films of '74

The year 1974 was a memorable one for Hollywood, with several iconic films hitting the silver screen. Here are some of the standout movies from that year:

Blazing Saddles

Mel Brooks directed this irreverent Western comedy that satirized the genre's tropes and racism. It became a cult classic known for its humor and social commentary.

Chinatown

Directed by Roman Polanski and starring Jack Nicholson and Faye Dunaway, this neo-noir film is considered one of the greatest in cinematic history. It was praised for its intricate plot and strong performances.

The Great Gatsby
Based on F. Scott Fitzgerald's novel, this adaptation starred Robert Redford as Jay Gatsby and Mia Farrow as Daisy Buchanan. It captured the opulence and disillusionment of the Roaring Twenties.

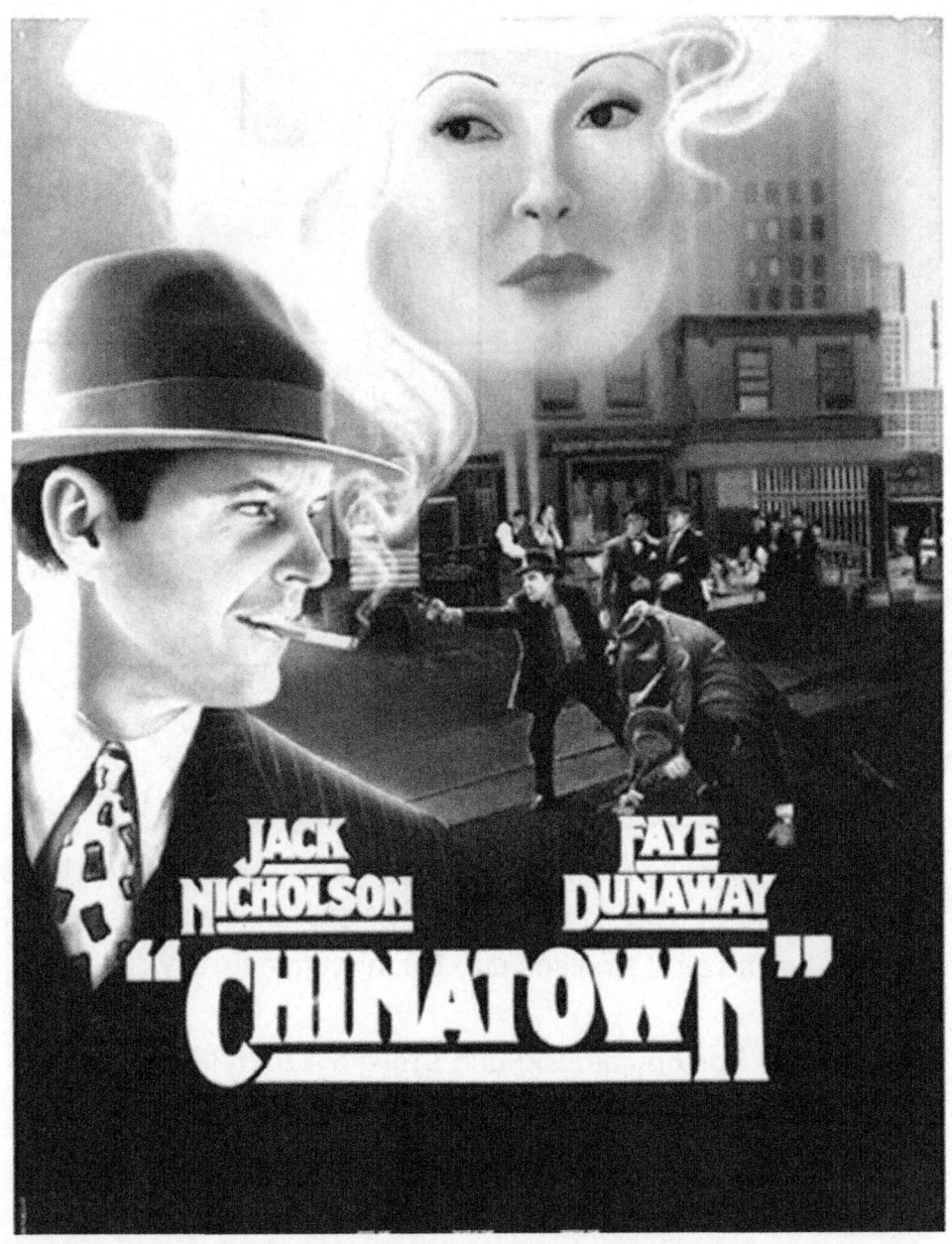

2.2 Small Screen Wonders: TV Shows That Captivated the Nation

Television in 1974 offered a diverse array of shows that captivated audiences across the nation. Here are a few TV shows that left a mark that year:

The Six Million Dollar Man

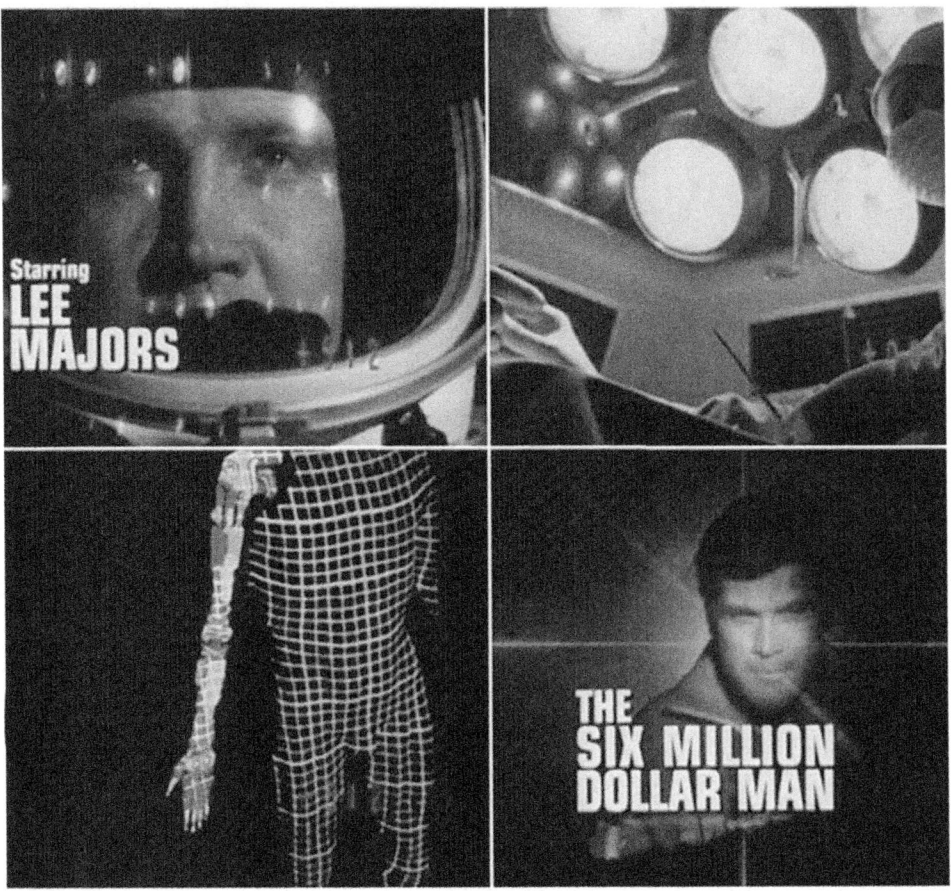

Starring Lee Majors, this science fiction series followed the adventures of Steve Austin, a bionic man with superhuman abilities. It was a hit and inspired spin-offs and merchandise.

Little House on the Prairie

Based on Laura Ingalls Wilder's books, this heartwarming series followed the lives of the Ingalls family as they settled in the American frontier during the late 1800s.

The Price Is Right

This long-running game show hosted by Bob Barker made its debut in 1974, challenging contestants to guess the prices of various products to win prizes.

2.3 The Red Carpet: Prestigious Film Awards and Honors

The film industry in 1974 was abuzz with prestigious awards and honors. Here are some of the notable accolades and ceremonies:

The 46th Academy Awards

The Oscars in 1974 honored outstanding achievements in film. "The Godfather Part II" dominated the awards, winning Best Picture, Best Director (Francis Ford Coppola), and Best Supporting Actor (Robert De Niro), among others.

The 32nd Primetime Emmy Awards

These awards celebrated excellence in television. "MAS*H" took home the Outstanding Comedy Series award, while "The Autobiography of Miss Jane Pittman" received accolades in the miniseries categories.

Cannes Film Festival

The 1974 Cannes Film Festival featured notable films like "The Conversation" by Francis Ford Coppola and "The Towering Inferno." The festival highlighted international cinema and awarded the prestigious Palme d'Or to "The Conversation."

Golden Globe Awards

The 31st Golden Globe Awards recognized excellence in both film and television. "Chinatown" won the award for Best Motion Picture – Drama, and Jack Nicholson received the Best Actor award for his role in the same film.

Grammy Awards

The Grammy Awards celebrated musical achievements in 1974. Roberta Flack's "Killing Me Softly with His Song" won Record of the Year, and Stevie Wonder's "Innervisions" won Album of the Year.

Activity: Movie and TV Show Trivia Quiz – How Well Do You Know '74 Entertainment?

Movie Trivia:

1. Who directed the iconic film "The Godfather Part II" in 1974?
2. In the 1974 film "Chinatown," who played the role of private investigator J.J. Gittes?
3. Which Mel Brooks comedy film from 1974 is a satirical take on the Western genre?
4. What F. Scott Fitzgerald novel was adapted into a film starring Robert Redford and Mia Farrow in 1974?
5. "Young Frankenstein," a 1974 comedy film, was directed by and starred whom?

TV Show Trivia:

1. Which 1974 sitcom is set in the 1950s and features the character known as "The Fonz"?
2. In the science fiction series "The Six Million Dollar Man," who portrayed the bionic man, Steve Austin?
3. What critically acclaimed 1974 TV series, set during the Korean War, blended comedy and drama in its portrayal of life at a mobile army surgical hospital?
4. "Little House on the Prairie," a popular TV series in 1974, is based on books written by whom?
5. What long-running game show, hosted by Bob Barker, made its debut in 1974 and involves guessing the prices of various products to win prizes?

Chapter 3: Music: Top Songs, Albums, and Awards

3.1 Renowned Musicians and Bands of '74

The year 1974 was a vibrant period for music, featuring a diverse range of renowned musicians and bands. Here are some of the notable artists who left their mark on the music scene in '74:

Elton John:

Elton John continued his meteoric rise in the music industry in 1974. Known for hits like "Bennie and the Jets" and "Don't Let the Sun Go Down on Me," he was a prominent figure in pop and rock music.

ABBA:

The Swedish pop group ABBA gained international recognition with their hit singles "Waterloo" and "Honey, Honey" in 1974, setting the stage for their global success.

Stevie Wonder:

Stevie Wonder was riding high on the success of his album "Fulfillingness' First Finale," which included hits like "Boogie On Reggae Woman" and "You Haven't Done Nothin'.

1974 A Time Traveler's Guide: Flashback Series of Memorial Books 26

David Bowie:

David Bowie continued to push musical boundaries with his album "Diamond Dogs." His alter ego, Ziggy Stardust, remained a cultural icon.

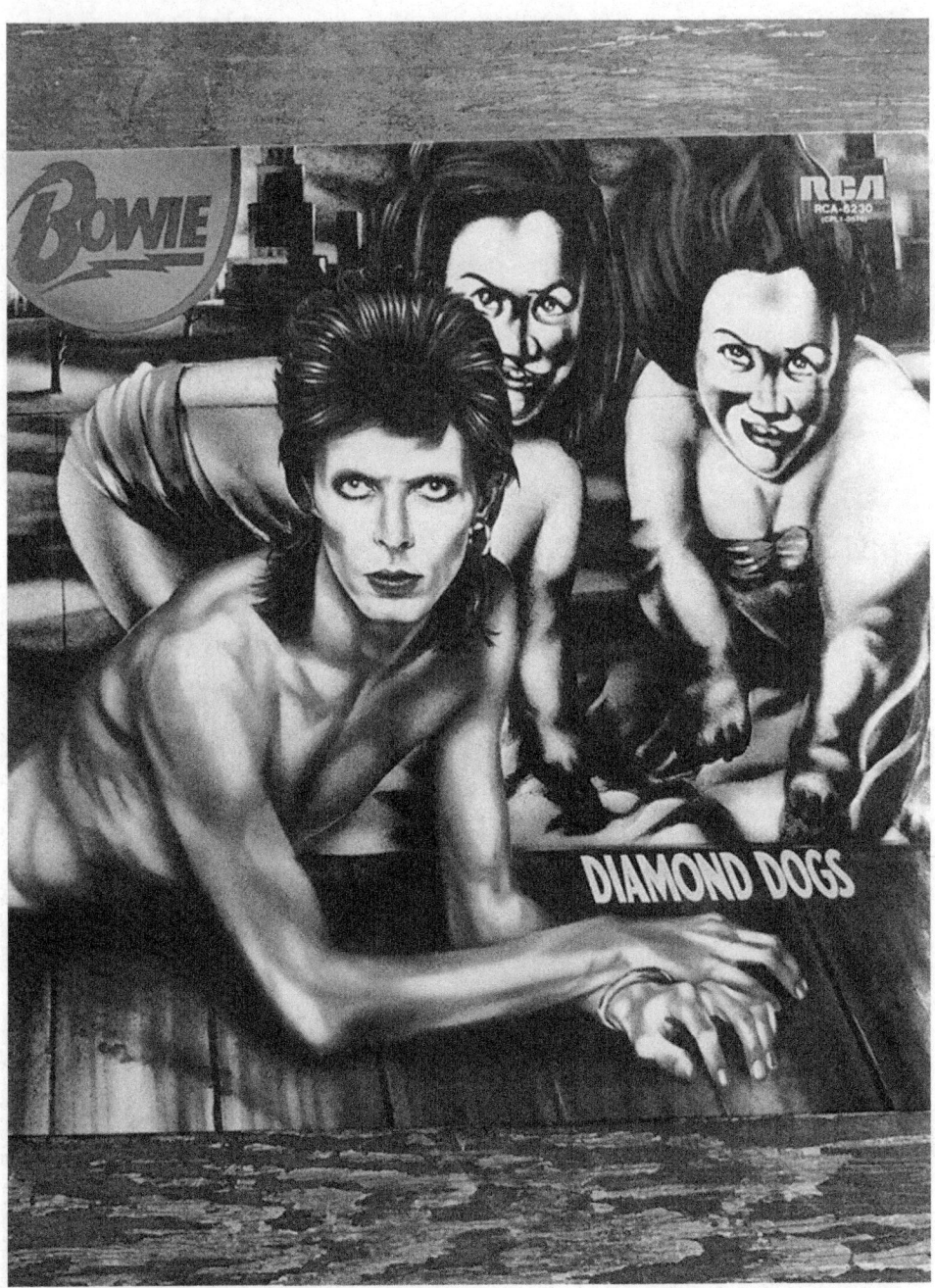

3.2 Notable Albums and Song Releases

1974 saw the release of several iconic albums and hit songs that left a lasting impact on the music industry:

"Court and Spark" by Joni Mitchell:

Joni Mitchell's album "Court and Spark" featured the hit single "Help Me" and showcased her unique blend of folk, rock, and jazz influences.

Band on the Run" by Paul McCartney & Wings:
This album by Paul McCartney & Wings produced classic tracks like the title song "Band on the Run" and "Jet."

"Dark Horse" by George Harrison:
Former Beatle George Harrison released "Dark Horse," featuring the hit song "Ding Dong, Ding Dong."

3.3 Music Awards and Honors

The world of music celebrated outstanding talent in 1974 through various awards and honors:

Grammy Awards:

The 16th Grammy Awards were held on 2nd March 1974, at Hollywood Palladium in Los Angeles. The Academy members presented the award to the artists for their superior performance for the 1973. Andy Williams was the anchor for the night. Stevie Wonder, Charlie Rich and Better Midler were the artists mostly nominated in all the categories for the year. The artist who grabbed the highest Grammys for the year was Stevie Wonder, winning a total of 5 Grammy Awards. Below is the list of winners for the year 1974.

1974 Grammy Awards

Record of the Year	"I Honestly Love You," Olivia Newton-John
Album of the Year	Fulfillingness' First Finale, Stevie Wonder (Tamla/Motown)
Song of the Year	"The Way We Were," Marilyn and Alan Bergman and Marvin Hamlisch, songwriters
Best New Artist of the Year	Marvin Hamlisch
Best Pop Vocal Performance, Male	Fulfillingness' First Finale, Stevie Wonder
Best Pop Vocal Performance, Female	"I Honestly Love You," Olivia Newton-John
Best Pop Vocal Performance By a Duo, Group or Chorus	"Band on the Run," Paul McCartney and Wings
Best Pop Instrumental Performance	"The Entertainer," Marvin Hamlisch
Best Rhythm and Blues Song	"Living for the City," Stevie Wonder, songwriter
Best Rhythm and Blues Vocal Performance, Male	"Boogie on Reggae Woman," Stevie Wonder
Best Rhythm and Blues Vocal Performance, Female	"Ain't Nothing Like the Real Thing," Aretha Franklin
Best Rhythm and Blues Vocal Performance By a Duo, Group or Chorus	"Tell Me Something Good," Rufus

Best Rhythm and Blues Instrumental Performance	"TSOP" (The Sound of Philadelphia), MFSB
Best Jazz Performance By a Soloist	First Recordings!, Charlie Parker
Best Jazz Performance By a Group	The Trio, Oscar Peterson, Joe Pass and Niels Pedersen
Best Jazz Performance By a Big Band	Thundering Herd, Woody Herman
Best Country Song	"A Very Special Love Song," Norris Wilson and Billy Sherrill, songwriters
Best Country Vocal Performance, Male	"Please Don't Tell Me How the Story Ends," Ronnie Milsap
Best Country Vocal Performance, Female	Love Song, Anne Murray
Best Country Vocal Performance By a Duo or Group	"Fairytale," Pointer Sisters
Best Country Instrumental Performance	The Atkins-Travis Traveling Show, Chet Atkins and Merle Travis
Best Gospel Performance	"The Baptism of Jesse Taylor," Oak Ridge Boys
Best Soul Gospel Performancet	In the Ghetto, James Cleveland and the Southern California Community Choir

Best Inspirational Performance	"How Great Thou Art," Elvis Presley
Best Ethnic or Traditional Recording	Two Days in November, Doc and Merle Watson
Best Instrumental Arrangement	"Threshold," Pat Williams, arranger
Best Arrangement Accompanying Vocalists	"Down to You," Joni Mitchell and Tom Scott, arrangers
Best Instrumental Composition	"Tubular Bells" (Theme From The Exorcist), Mike Oldfield, composer
Best Score From an Original Cast Show Album	Raisin, Judd Woldin and Robert Britten, composers (Columbia)
Album of Best Original Score Written for a Motion Picture or a Television Special	The Way We Were, Marvin Hamlisch and Alan and Marilyn Bergman, composers (Columbia)
Album of the Year, Classical	Berlioz, Symphonie Fantastique, Sir Georg Solti conducting Chicago Symphony (London)
Best Classical Performance, Orchestra	Berlioz, Symphonie Fantastique, Sir Georg Solti conducting Chicago Symphony
Best Chamber Music Performance	Brahms and Schumann Trios, Artur Rubinstein, Henryk Szeryng and Pierre Fournier

Best Classical Performance, Instrumental Soloist(s) (With Orchestra)	Shostakovich, Violin Concerto No. 1, David Oistrakh
Best Classical Performance, Instrumental Soloist(s) (Without Orchestra)	Albeniz, Iberia, Alicia de Larrocha
Best Opera Recording	Puccini, La Bohème, Sir Georg Solti conducting London Philharmonic; solos: Caballé, Domingo, Milnes, Blegen and Raimondi (RCA)
Best Choral Performance, Classical (Other Than Opera)	Berlioz, The Damnation of Faust, Colin Davis conducting London Symphony Orchestra and Chorus, Ambrosian Singers and Wandsworth School Boys' Choir; solos: Gedda, Bastin, Veasey and Van Allen
Best Classical Vocal Soloist Performance	Leontyne Price Sings Richard Strauss, Leontyne Price
Best Comedy Recording	That Nigger's Crazy, Richard Pryor (Partee/Stax)
Best Spoken Word Recording	Good Evening, Peter Cook and Dudley Moore (Island)
Best Recording for Childrent	Winnie the Pooh and Tigger Too, Sebastian Cabot, Sterling Holloway and Paul Winchell (Disneyland)

Best Album Package	Come and Gone, Ed Thrasher and Christopher Whorf, art directors (Warner Bros.)
Best Album Notes (tie)	For the Last Time, Charles R. Townsend, annotator (United Artists)
	The Hawk Flies, Dan Morgenstern, annotator (Milestone)
Best Album Notes, Classical	The Classic Erich Wolfgang Korngold, Rory Guy, annotator (Angel)
Best Producer of the Year	Thom Bell

Activity: Music Lyrics Challenge - Guess the Song Lyrics from '74

Activity: Music Lyrics Challenge - Guess the Song Lyrics from '74

Let's test your knowledge of music from 1974 with a lyrics challenge! Can you guess the song lyrics from the iconic track "Band on the Run" by Paul McCartney & Wings? Fill in the missing words from the lyrics below:

Lyrics:
Stuck _____ in the road
You would've _____, but you're too slow
Those last two verses, I know they're a waste
But I like to write 'em, it helps me get it straight
You're the _____ I've ever seen
You can talk to me
You can talk to me
You can talk to me
If you're down and _____ (ooh)
If you're on the ground (ooh)
Baby, I'm aware
Of where you go
What do we hope to find?
Inside the _____?
You know we're not so far from _____
So let's see what we can find
Give it _____, I know we can make it work out
I can see it in your eyes (ooh)
Do you see it in mine? (ooh)
I can see it in your eyes
I can see it in your eyes
I can see it in your eyes
I can see it in your eyes
Now you're looking at me
And you're _____ your head
And I'm trying to see you, baby
But I'm _____, I'm just aching instead
'Cause you're the _____ I've ever seen
You can talk to me
You can talk to me

You can talk to me
You can talk to me
If you're down and lost (ooh)
If you're on the run (ooh)
Baby, I'm aware
Of where you go (ooh)
What do we hope to find?
Inside the _____?
You know we're not so far from _____
So let's see what we can find
Give it _____, I know we can make it work out
I can see it in your eyes (ooh)
Do you see it in mine? (ooh)
I can see it in your eyes (ooh)
I can see it in your eyes (ooh)
I can see it in your eyes (ooh)
I can see it in your eyes (ooh)
Fill in the Missing Words:
Stuck _____ in the road
You would've _____, but you're too slow
Those last two verses, I know they're a waste
But I like to write 'em, it helps me get it straight
You're the _____ I've ever seen
You can talk to me
You can talk to me
You can talk to me
If you're down and _____ (ooh)
If you're on the ground (ooh)
Baby, I'm aware
Of where you go

What do we hope to find?
Inside the _____?
You know we're not so far from _____
So let's see what we can find
Give it _____, I know we can make it work out
I can see it in your eyes (ooh)
Do you see it in mine? (ooh)
I can see it in your eyes
I can see it in your eyes
I can see it in your eyes
I can see it in your eyes
Now you're looking at me
And you're _____ your head
And I'm trying to see you, baby
But I'm _____, I'm just aching instead
'Cause you're the _____ I've ever seen
You can talk to me
You can talk to me
You can talk to me
If you're down and lost (ooh)
If you're on the run (ooh)
Baby, I'm aware
Of where you go (ooh)
What do we hope to find?
Inside the _____?
You know we're not so far from _____
So let's see what we can find
Give it _____, I know we can make it work out
I can see it in your eyes (ooh)
Do you see it in mine? (ooh)
I can see it in your eyes (ooh)
I can see it in your eyes (ooh)

I can see it in your eyes (ooh)
I can see it in your eyes (ooh)
Take a moment to fill in the missing words and see how well you remember the lyrics from "Band on the Run" by Paul McCartney & Wings!

Chapter 4: Sporting Highlights for 1974

Here are some of the sporting highlights in the world of sport for 1974.

Football

The major events of the year were the FIFA World Cup, won by hosts Germany, and the Commonwealth Games (called the British Commonwealth Games) in New Zealand.

It was the 10th edition of the FIFA World Cup in which the host nation West Germany defeated the Netherlands by 2-1.

Basketball

UCLA was riding an 88-game winning streak, which started three years ago in 1971, heading into a match against Notre Dame which they lost to bring the longest streak ever in NCAA history to an end. The streak stood as the longest in college sports until UConn women's basketball team put together a 90 game win streak.

Tennis

Chris Evert won her first grand slam as a 19yr old at the French Open and immediately followed it up with a Wimbledon win en-route to a stellar career with 18 grand slam titles. Jimmy Connors had a spectacular year with three grand slam titles. He was not allowed to participate in the French Open that year which he would not play in until 1978. He reached the world no.1 ranking in July that year after his Wimbledon win which he retained for a then record of 160 weeks.

Golf

Sandra Haynie won the LPGA Championship and U.S. Women's Open for her third and fourth major. Gary Player who had already won six majors till then took the Masters Tournament and The Open Championship. He would finish his career with a total of eight majors. Lee Trevino won the PGA Championship for the fifth out of his six total major wins.

1974

Below is a timeline of some significant results in the world of sport for the year 1974.

Date	Results
Jan	Tennis Australia Open won by Jimmy Connors and Evonne Goolagong
Jan 24 - Feb 2	Commonwealth Games held in Christchurch, New Zealand.
Feb	Super Bowl held in Houston won by Miami
April	Golf Masters won by Gary Player (2nd win)
May	Tennis French Open won by Bjorn Borg and Chris Evert
June	Golf US Open won by Hale Irwin
June 13 - July 7	FIFA World Cup (Football) tournament was held in Germany, won by Germany.
July	the Cycling Tour de France won by Eddy Merckx
July	Tennis Wimbledon won by Jimmy Connors and Chris Evert
July	Golf The Open Championship won by Gary Player
Aug	Golf US PGA won by Lee Trevino
Sep	Tennis US Open won by Jimmy Connors and Billie Jean King
Oct	The Baseball World Series won by Oakland Athletics

Activity: Sports Trivia
Test Your Knowledge of 1974 Sports History

Let's test your knowledge of sports history in 1974! See if you can answer these questions based on the sports events and results from that year.

Football:

Which nation hosted and won the 1974 FIFA World Cup?
a) Brazil
b) West Germany
c) Argentina
d) Italy

In the 1974 FIFA World Cup final, which team did West Germany defeat, and what was the final score?
a) Netherlands, 3-1
b) Argentina, 2-0
c) Brazil, 4-2
d) Italy, 2-1

Basketball:

What university's basketball team had an 88-game winning streak in 1974, and who ended that streak with a victory?
a) University of North Carolina, Duke University
b) UCLA, Notre Dame
c) Kentucky, Indiana
d) Michigan State, Michigan

How many consecutive games did the UConn women's basketball team win to break the previous NCAA record?
a) 75
b) 82
c) 90
d) 100

Tennis:

5. Who won her first grand slam title at the 1974 French Open, and how old was she at the time?
a) Serena Williams, 17
b) Martina Navratilova, 19
c) Chris Evert, 19
d) Steffi Graf, 18

6. Which male tennis player had a spectacular year in 1974, winning three grand slam titles?
a) Bjorn Borg
b) Roger Federer
c) Rafael Nadal
d) Jimmy Connors

7. Who reached the world No. 1 ranking in July 1974 after winning Wimbledon and held that ranking for a then-record number of weeks?
a) Rod Laver
b) Pete Sampras
c) John McEnroe
d) Jimmy Connors

Golf:

8. In golf, who won the LPGA Championship and U.S. Women's Open in 1974, securing her third and fourth major titles?
a) Annika Sorenstam
b) Nancy Lopez
c) Sandra Haynie
d) Laura Davies

9. How many major titles did Gary Player have before winning the Masters Tournament and The Open Championship in 1974?
a) Four
b) Five
c) Six
d) Seven

10. Which golfer secured his fifth PGA Championship win in 1974, out of a total of six major victories?
a) Jack Nicklaus
b) Arnold Palmer
c) Tom Watson
d) Lee Trevino

Feel free to select the letter corresponding to your answer for each question, and then check your answers later.

Chapter 5:
Fashion, and Popular LeisureActivities

5.1 Fashion Flashback: What the World Wore in '74

The year 1974 was a fascinating time for fashion, marked by a blend of nostalgic throwbacks and bold, innovative styles. Let's take a journey back in time to explore the fashion trends and iconic looks that defined the year:
The prices shown for these Fashion Clothing are the price they were sold for in 1974 not today

Checked Separates

Price: $21.00 - $38.00

Description Peppy separates check out in a cotton skirt, navy/white with red woven stripe or red/white with navy woven stripe; and polyester/cotton shirt in red/white or navy/white.

Cotton Madras Shirt

Price: $25.00

Description Gant Indian cotton madras shirt is created of multicolor patches sewn together. Long sleeves have one-button cuffs. Shirt back is yoked with a box pleat for easy movement.

Damon Cardigan

Price: $27.50

Description Damon cardigan of bird's-eye acrylic with striking striped binding, waist and cuffs. In taupe or navy.

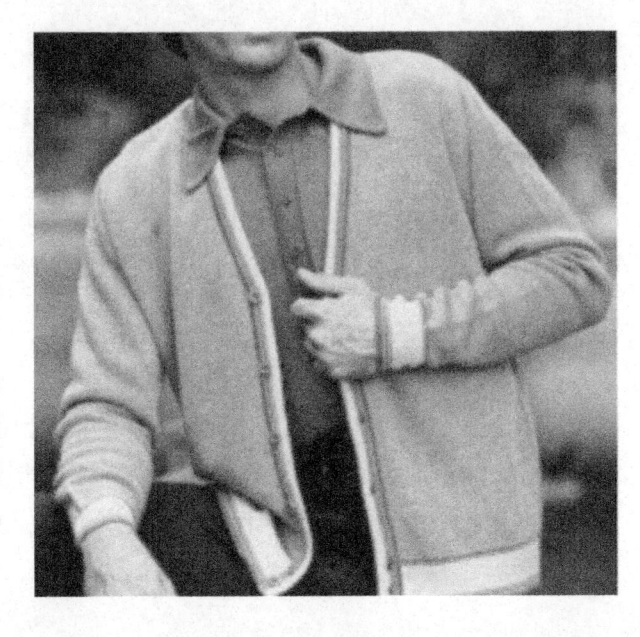

Donald Brooks Fur Coat
Price: $4,500.00
Description By Donald Brooks, natural chestnut mink with fitted back, bias-cut puffed sleeves. Fluffy, tip-dyed Russian sable collar. Suede belt.

Geometric Sport Shirt
Price: $25.00
Description Damon's geometric sport shirt is a bold print on nylon twill. Natural ground.

Green Paisley Shirt/ $25.00
Description Adelaar green paisley polyester shirt has a matching long flip tie to wear under your collar or around the neck or head. Yoke back, long sleeves with one-button cuffs, rounded hemline.

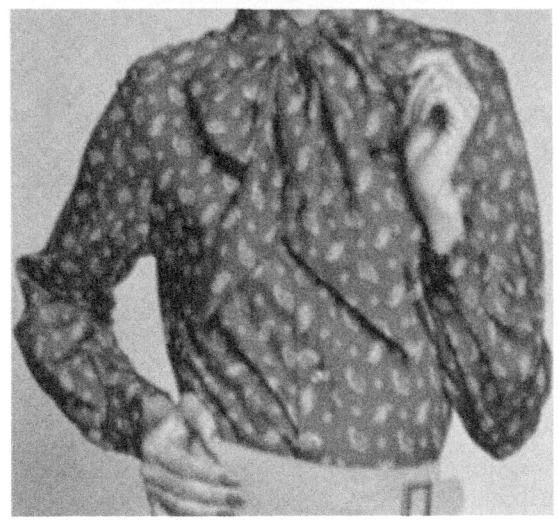

1974 A Time Traveler's Guide: Flashback Series of Memorial Books 50

Hooded Coat
Price: $135.00
Description Rugged shelter for the life he leads. Fox Trot hooded duffle coat by Zero King is acrylic/modacrylic pile on cotton back. Wool/nylon lining. Red fox color.

Hooded Wool Cardigan
Price: $70.00
Description South American hooded wool cardigan, hand-made in Ecuador, is distinctive with an unusual design on the textured hood, cardigan front, sleeve edges, pockets and hemline. Raglan sleeves, soft self-tie belt, buttons shaped like Brazil nuts. Natural color with brown accents.

Nylon Sport Shirt
Price: $28.50
Description DuPont Qiana nylon sport shirt. Confetti-dotted circles on dark ground. Comes in navy or brown.

Pauline Trigere Holiday Gown
Price: $700.00
Description Pauline Trigere touches this beautifully-cut wool jersey holiday gown with crescendos of rhinestones.

Plaid Shirt
Price: $24.00
Description Pendleton red plaid shirt of wool boasts classic lines, fine tailoring.

Polo and Seersucker Culotte

Price: $14.00 - $26.00

Description Polo shirt of cotton and polyester by Leon Levin has button front placket, short sleeves. In refreshing lime, yellow or white. Zip-open cotton seersucker culotte by Leon Levin is shorts and skirt in one. Comes in white/green/yellow plaid.

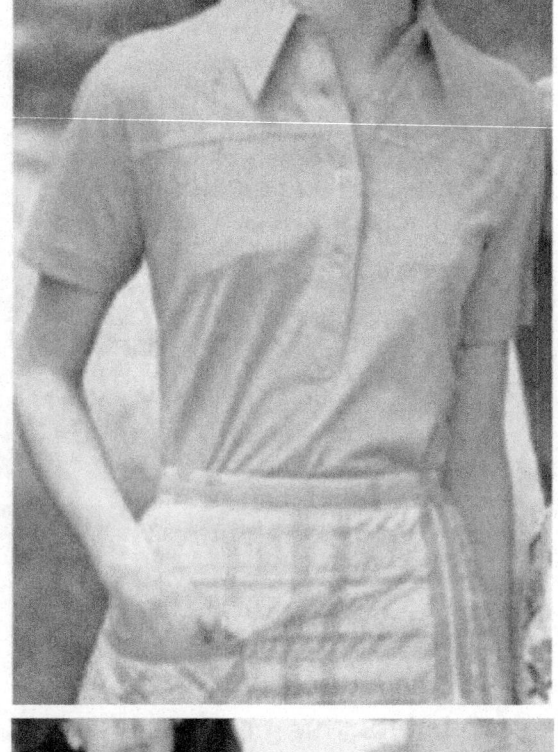

Polyester Chiffon Dress

Price: $36.00 - $48.00

Description Floating partners in double-layer polyester chiffon by Malbe. American beauty or coffee brown. The overblouse has a price of $36.00, the skirt has a price of $48.00.

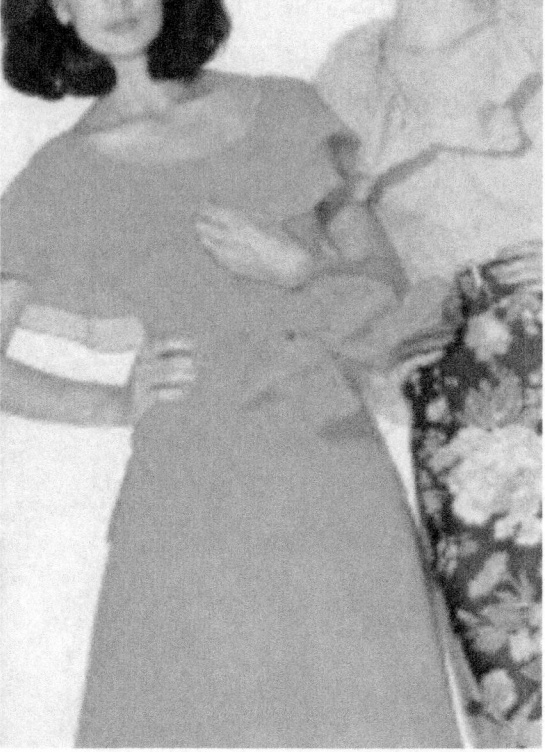

Swimwear with Cover-Up
Price: $7.00 - $38.00
Description Beached, in the Tahitian manner: swimwear by Tom Brigance. One-shoulder mailot ($32.00) in nylon/Lycra spandex; draped long-skirt coverup ($38.00) with side thigh slit, also worn as one-shoulder coverup. Triangle scarf ($7.00) measures 47x32x32 inches and shields hair from sun or slips over shoulders. Skirt, scarf in nylon jersey. All in blue Tahiti print.

5.2 Leisure Pursuits: Entertainment and Hobbies

The Rise of Rubik's Cube: While the Rubik's Cube was nvented in 1974, it would later become a worldwide sensation, challenging minds and dexterity in the realm of puzzles and brain teasers.

Lego Sets: Lego sets continued to capture the imaginations of children and adults, offering endless possibilities for creative construction.

"Jaws" by Peter Benchley: The novel "Jaws," released in 1974, would go on to inspire Steven Spielberg's blockbuster film. It tapped into primal fears of the deep sea and the relentless great white shark.

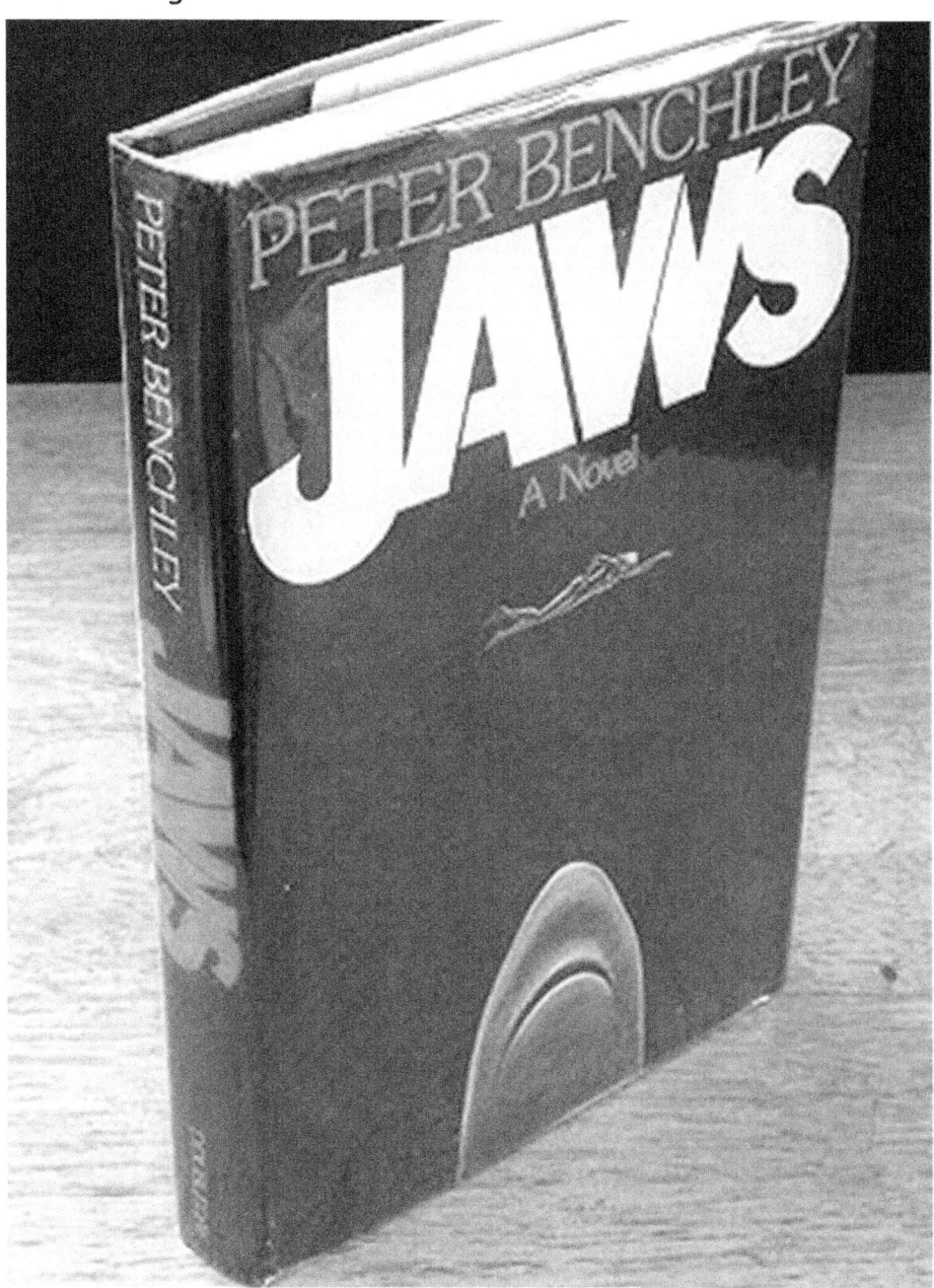

1974 A Time Traveler's Guide: Flashback Series of Memorial Books 56

Board Games and Toys:
Board games like "Risk" and "Clue" continued to be popular choices for family entertainment.

Action figures, including G.I. Joe and Barbie, remained beloved toys for children and collectors alike.

1974 A Time Traveler's Guide: Flashback Series of Memorial Books 57

Activity:
Fashion Design Coloring Page
-Create Your '74-Inspired Outfit

1974 A Time Traveler's Guide: Flashback Series of Memorial Books 58

1974 Marjorie Hackett's "Women's Traditional" Uniform

1974 Uniform (Pantsuit Option)

Chapter 6: Technological Advancements and Popular Cars

6.1 Innovations That Shaped the Future

The year 1974 witnessed several groundbreaking innovations and technological advancements that played a significant role in shaping the future. Let's explore some of the key innovations from that transformative year:

1. Personal Computer Revolution:

Intel 8080 Microprocessor: Intel's release of the 8080 microprocessor marked a pivotal moment in computing history. This microprocessor, along with the Altair 8800 computer, sparked the birth of the personal computer revolution.

Altair 8800: Developed by Micro Instrumentation and Telemetry Systems (MITS), the Altair 8800 was one of the first widely available microcomputers, providing hobbyists and early computer enthusiasts with a platform to experiment and program.

2. Ethernet and Networking:

Ethernet Standardization: Ethernet, a key technology for local area networking (LAN), took a major step forward in 1974 when Robert Metcalfe and David Boggs at Xerox PARC published their Ethernet paper. This laid the foundation for the Ethernet standard we use for networking today.

3. Space Exploration:

Skylab Space Station: Skylab, the United States' first space station, was launched in 1973 but remained active throughout 1974. It hosted scientific experiments, observations, and studies that contributed to our understanding of space and human adaptation to extended spaceflight.

4. Medical Advancements:

MRI Technology: The first MRI (Magnetic Resonance Imaging) scanner was introduced in 1974. This revolutionary medical imaging technology provided non-invasive, high-resolution images of the body's internal structures, revolutionizing diagnosis and research.

Cancer Found Electronically

Distinct Signals Sent by Atoms From Cells

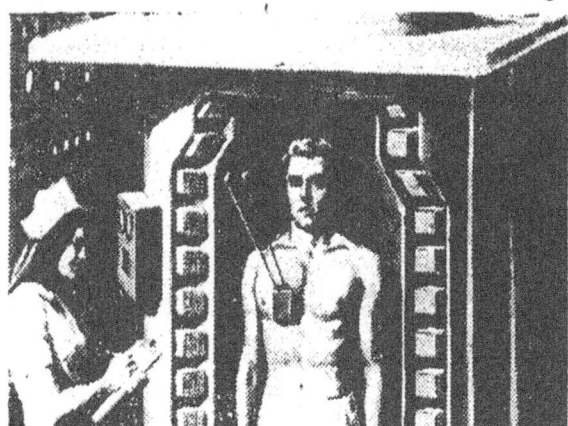

These innovations of 1974 not only shaped the immediate future but also laid the groundwork for the technological and scientific advancements that continue to shape our lives today. From the birth of personal computing to breakthroughs in medical technology and space exploration, this year marked a pivotal moment in the trajectory of human progress and innovation.

6.2 The Automobiles of '74

In 1974, the automotive industry released several standouts. While most can't be found on the road today, they were influential in shaping the industry and spawned the next generation of cars.

Here are five of the best cars of 1974 that are worth remembering.

1.The best car of 1974: Ford Pinto

Original MSRP: $2,771

Powertrain: 80-horsepower, 2.3L I-4 engine with 4-speed manual or 3-speed automatic transmission

What makes it special:

In its heyday, the Ford Pinto was praised for its reliability and low repair costs. Plus, this subcompact got 20 mpg, which was considered quite good for the mid-'70s.

But it didn't win over everyone. Critics complained about its lack of quality, even though defects were few and far between.

The popular Pinto was safe (by most accounts) and boasted an innovative exterior and nice handling. Consider yourself lucky if you ever got the chance to drive one of these iconic beauties.

2. The best hatchback of 1974: Simca 1100 Ti

Powertrain: 82-horsepower I-4 engine with 4-speed manual transmission

What makes it special:
When people think of hatchbacks, they often think of Volkswagen. Most people don't realize that the Golf debuted two years after the release of the somewhat forgotten Simca.
French automaker Simca had been around since 1967. At the time, its vehicles were quiteadvanced, thanks to disc brakes, rack and pinion steering, and all-round independent suspension.
Upon release, the Simca 1100 was a huge hit, and Volkswagen used it as a case study to create the Golf.
1974 saw the launch of the Ti model with a 1.3-liter engine. It could reach a top speed of 105 mph and go 0 to 60 in 12 seconds, sealing its fate as one of the best cars of 1974.

3. The best luxury car of 1974: Lamborghini Countach LP 400 Periscopio

Original MSRP: $52,000
Powertrain: 345-horsepower, 3.9L V12 with 5-speed manual transmission
What makes it special:
It's probably not a huge surprise to most people that Lamborghini made the best sports car of 1974. The Countach played a big part in launching the global popularity of the supercar.

Its wedge-shaped body set a trend that other supercars would follow for decades. The most iconic version came in Argento silver with a tobacco brown interior. These two style choices combined to create a stunning look inside and out.

4. The best family car of 1974: Chevrolet Impala

Original MSRP: $4,229
Powertrain: 145-horsepower, 350 Turbo Jet V8 engine with 3-speed automatic transmission
What makes it special:
In 1974, the Chevrolet Impala could be found in many suburban driveways. It was reliable, had a spacious interior, and held its value well.

The '74 Impala wasn't just a popular car, it ingrained itself in American culture. Its unique body and lowered stance made it stand out from rivals.

While many car lovers will go on and on about its style and drivability, the fact it was proven to be especially safe on the road made it popular among families.

Unsurprisingly, modern versions of the Impala are still selling well in the United States today.

5. The best full-sized muscle car of 1974: Dodge Monaco

Original MSRP: $4,259
Powertrain: 220-horsepower, 5.9L V8 with 3-speed automatic transmission
What makes it special:
Granted, the Dodge Monaco is too big to be a "true" muscle car. That said, it had enough power to keep pace with the best of them.
The Monaco was redesigned in 1974 with a unibody platform and all-new sheet metal. The fact it didn't sell well is partly attributed to the 1970s oil crisis. Bigger cars suffered the most, and Chrysler took some flack for still producing them. The Dodge Monaco was fast and aggressive—barreling down the road, often scaring other drivers. It also induced a lot of awe.

Activity: Classic Car Match-Up
Test Your Knowledge of 1974's Best Cars

Let's dive into the world of classic cars from 1974. Take a trip down memory lane and see if you can match the cars with their names based on the information provided in the book.

Instructions:

Read the descriptions of the five iconic cars from 1974. Match each car's description with its correct name from the list below.

Write the corresponding car name (1 to 5) next to each description.

Car Names:

Ford Pinto
Simca 1100 Ti
Lamborghini Countach LP 400 Periscopio
Chevrolet Impala
Dodge Monaco

Car Descriptions:

A. Known for its reliability and low repair costs, this subcompact was a popular choice in the mid-'70s. It offered good fuel efficiency and was considered a safe option. Critics complained about its quality, but defects were rare.

B. This hatchback was somewhat forgotten but paved the way for cars like the Volkswagen Golf. It boasted advanced features for its time, including disc brakes, rack and pinion steering, and independent suspension. In 1974, a Ti model with a 1.3-liter engine made waves.

C. This luxury car was a true sports car icon of 1974. With its wedge-shaped body, it set trends that supercars would follow for decades. The most iconic version came in Argento silver with a tobacco brown interior, creating a stunning look inside and out.

D. A common sight in suburban driveways, this family car was known for its reliability, spacious interior, and strong resale value. Its unique body and lowered stance made it stand out, and it earned a reputation for safety.

E. While not a traditional muscle car due to its size, this car had enough power to rival the best of them. The 1974 redesign featured a unibody platform and new sheet metal. Despite the '70s oil crisis, it remained fast and aggressive on the road.

Now, see how many matches you can make. Check your answers below:

Answers:
A. ………………………..
B. ……………………….
C. ………………………
D. ………………………
E. ………………………

Let's see how well you know your classic cars from 1974!

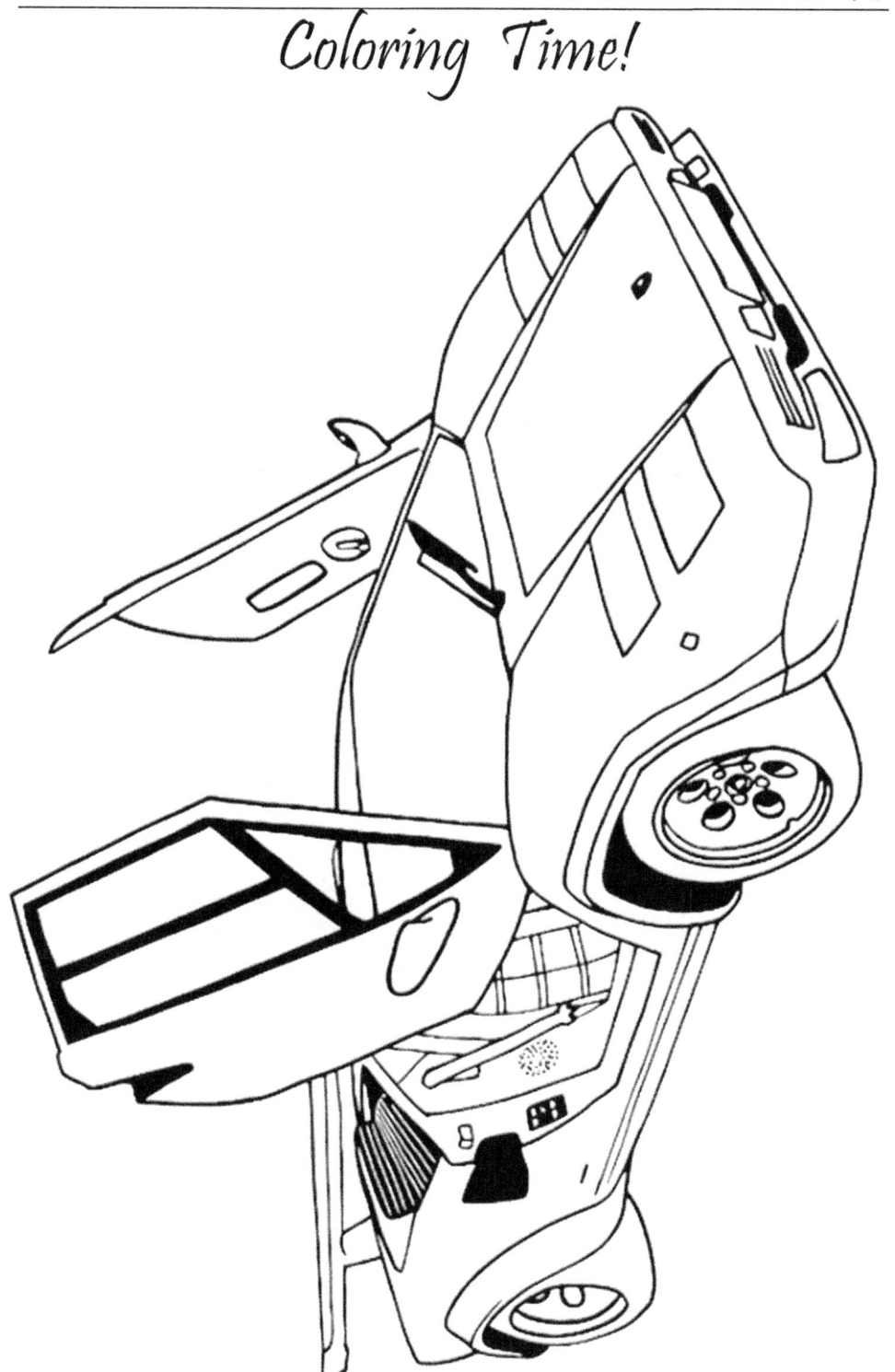

1974   A Time Traveler's Guide: Flashback Series of Memorial Books   71

Coloring Time!

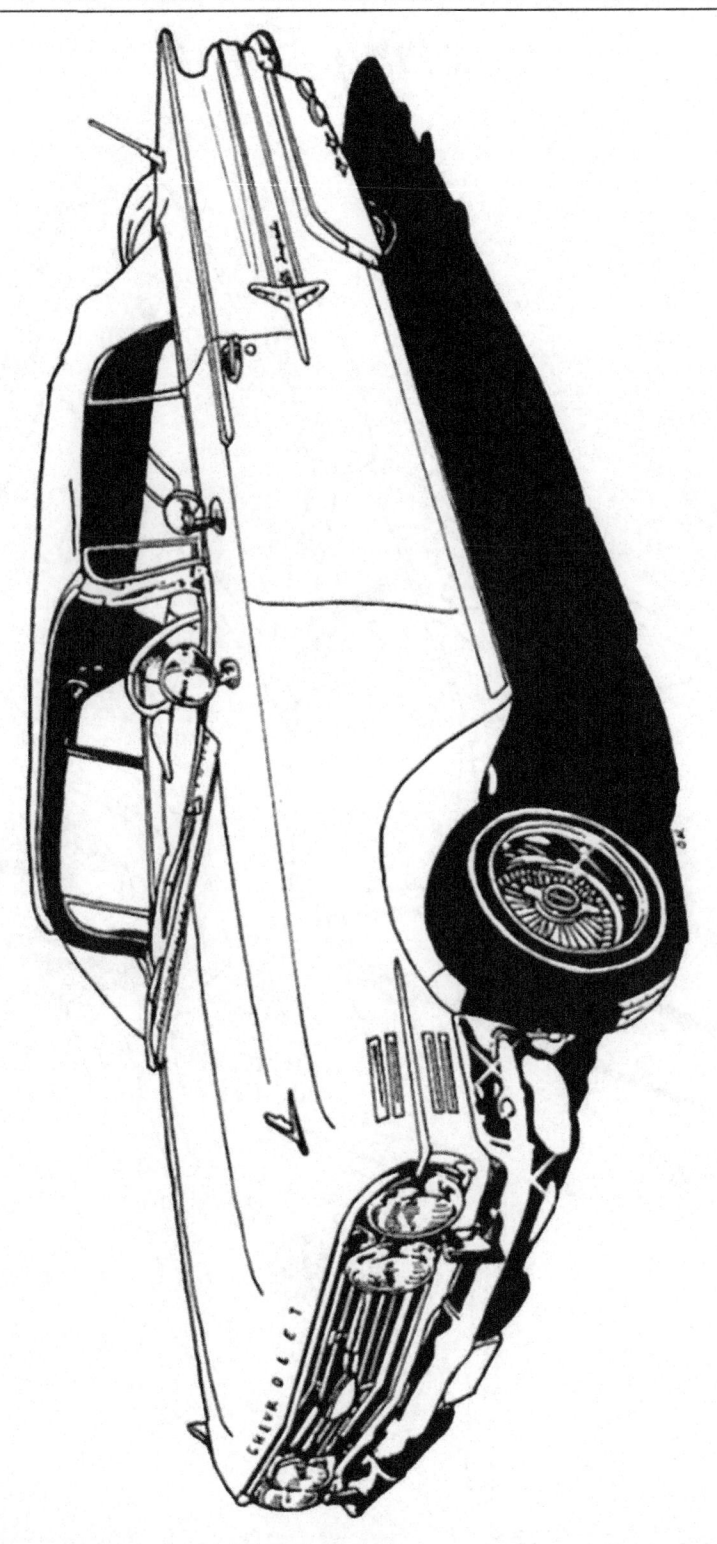

1974 A Time Traveler's Guide: Flashback Series of Memorial Books 72

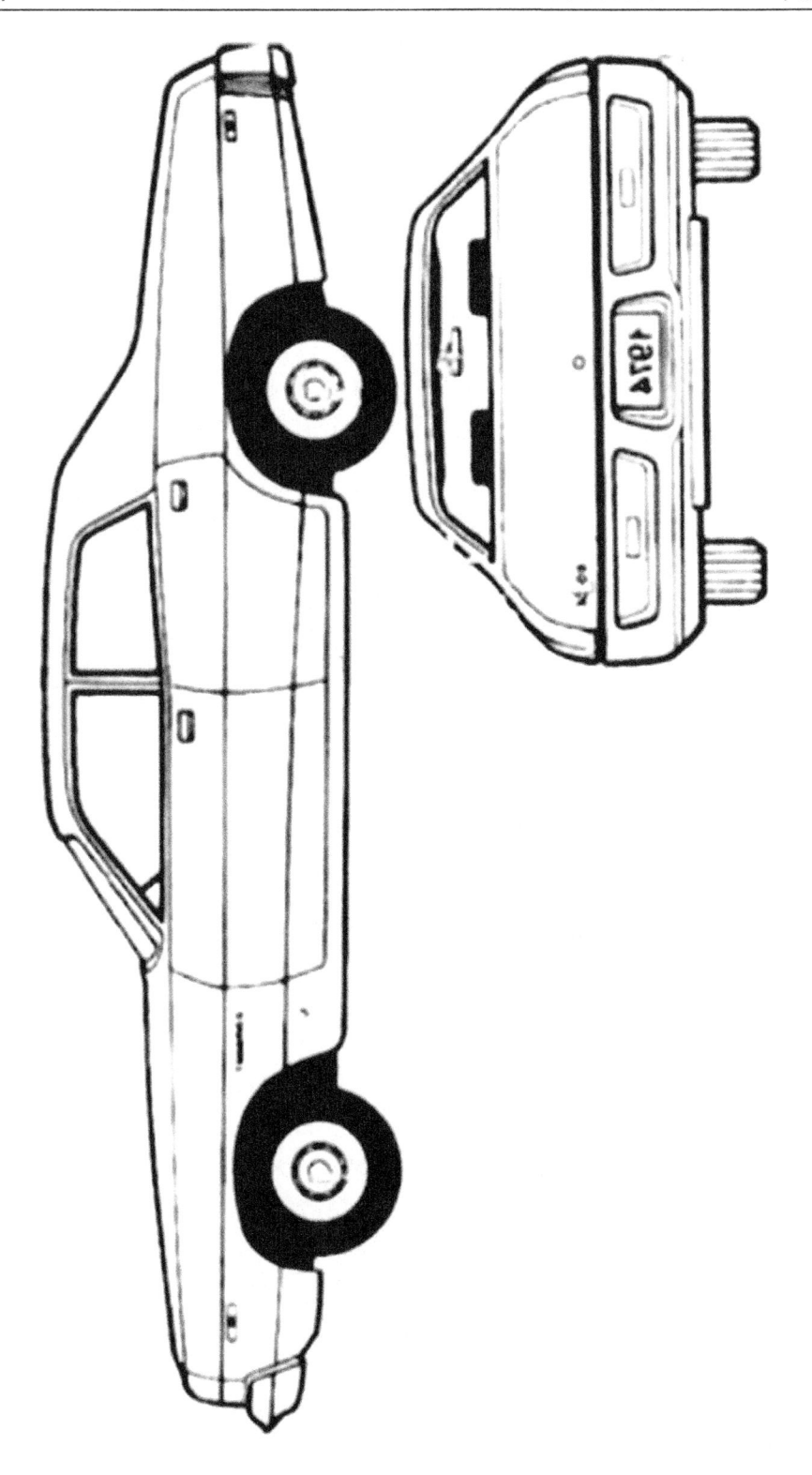

1974 A Time Traveler's Guide: Flashback Series of Memorial Books 73

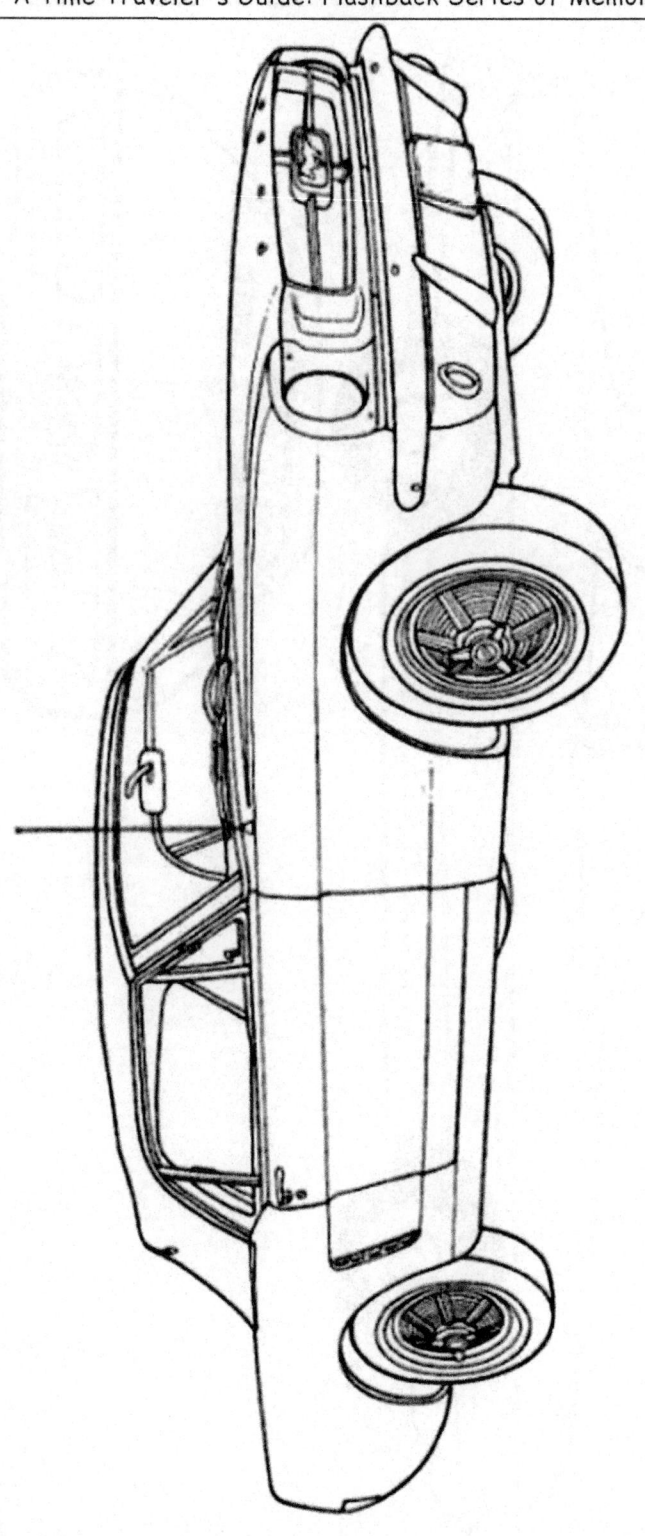

1974 A Time Traveler's Guide: Flashback Series of Memorial Books 74

Chapter 7: The Cost of Things

7.1 The Cost of Living in 1974

HOW MUCH THINGS COST IN 1974

Yearly Inflation Rate USA	11.3%
Yearly Inflation Rate UK	17.2%
Average Income per year	$13,900.00
Average Cost of new house	$34,900.00
Buick Station Wagon	$4,371
Average Monthly Rent	$185.00
Country ranch 10 acres 3 bedroom large barn fruit and oak trees Vallejo -- California	$59,200

Grocery Prices Jump to Highest Mark Since 1974

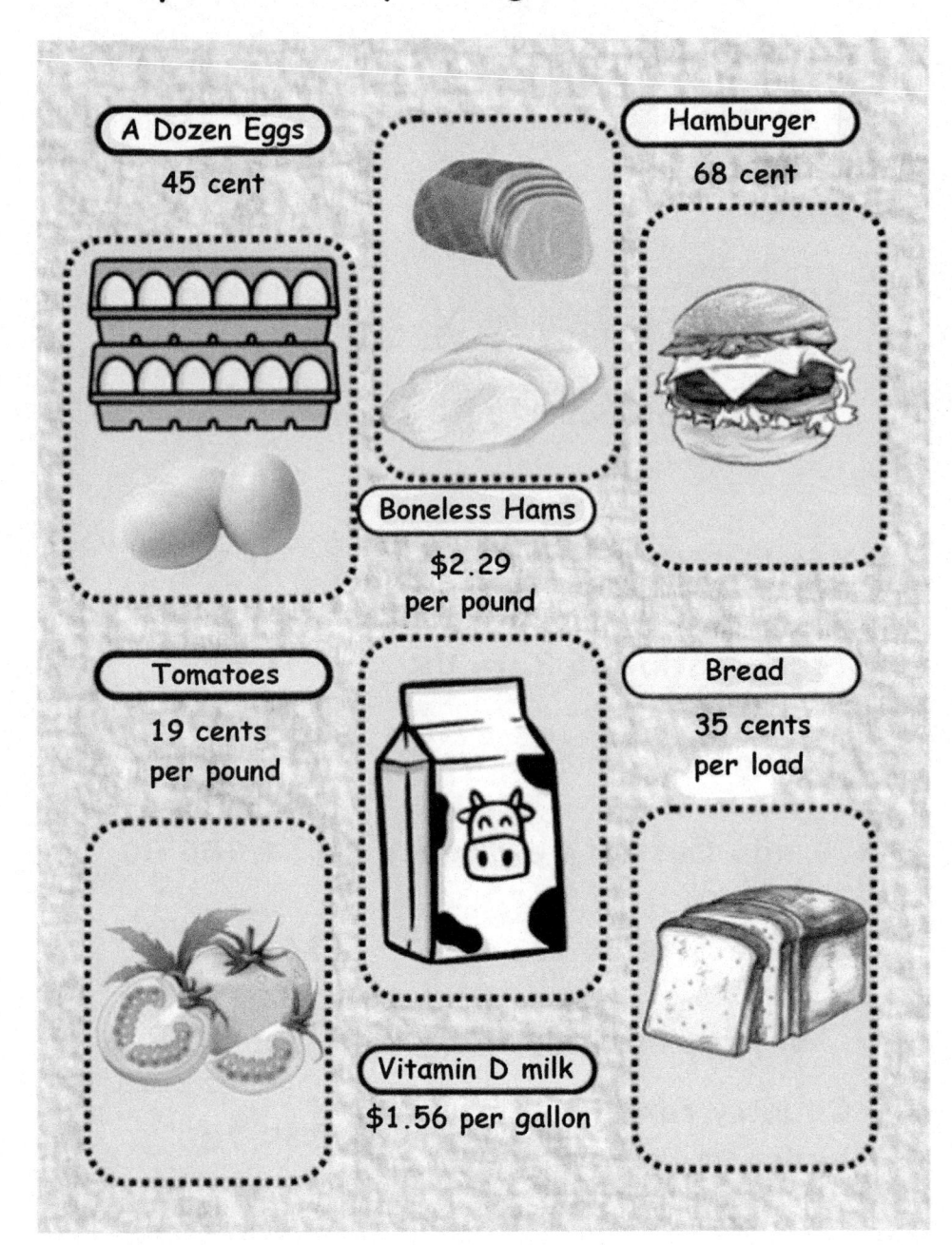

A Dozen Eggs
45 cent

Hamburger
68 cent

Boneless Hams
$2.29 per pound

Tomatoes
19 cents per pound

Bread
35 cents per load

Vitamin D milk
$1.56 per gallon

1974

Other thing's prices

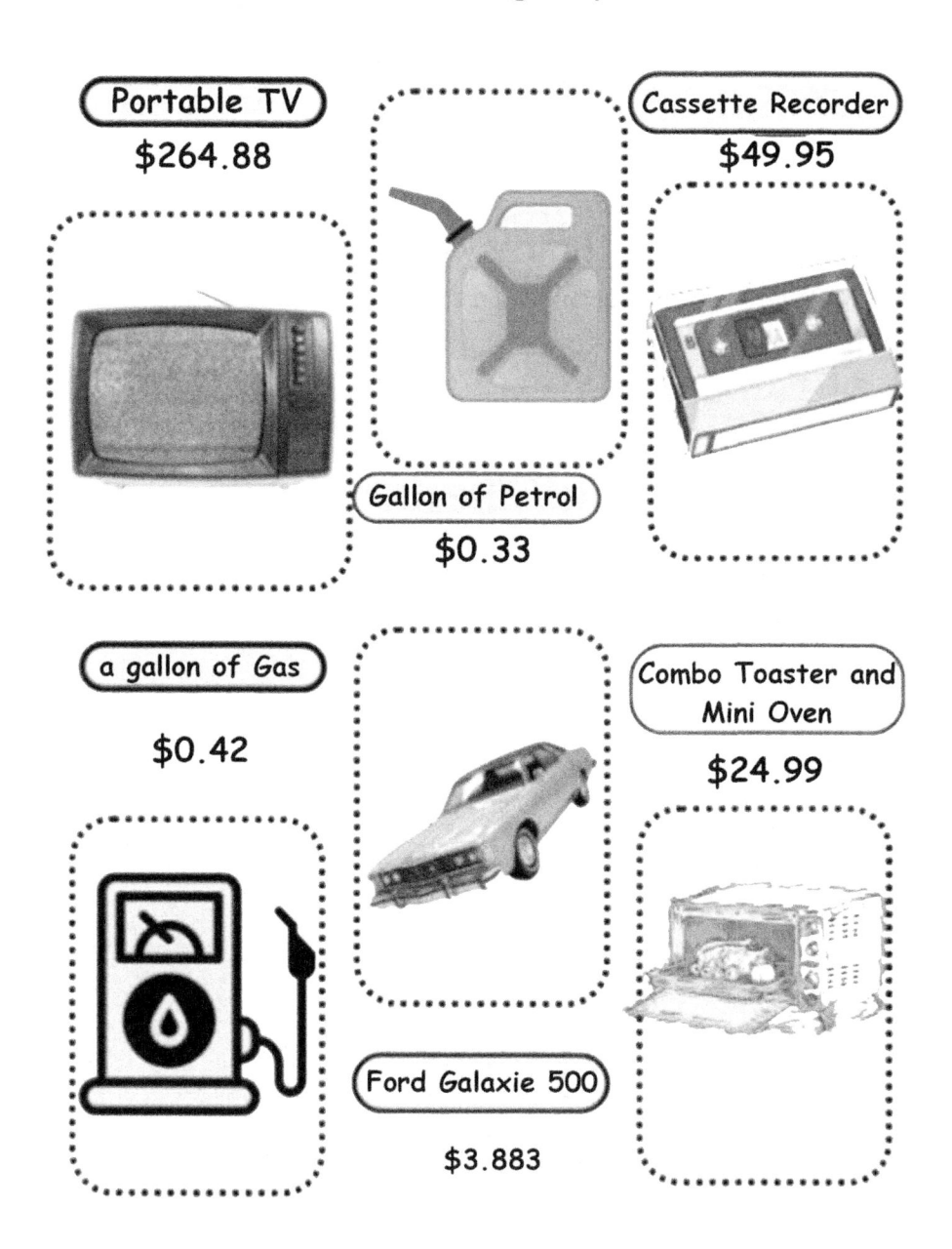

Portable TV
$264.88

Cassette Recorder
$49.95

Gallon of Petrol
$0.33

a gallon of Gas
$0.42

Combo Toaster and Mini Oven
$24.99

Ford Galaxie 500
$3.883

Activity: 1974 Shopping List Challenge

Let's take a step back in time to 1974 and explore what a shopping list might have looked like during that era. This activity will give you a taste of the products and items that were popular and essential back in the '70s. Try to guess what would have been on a typical shopping list for a family in 1974.

Instructions:

Imagine you're a household shopper in 1974.

Review the information from the book about trends, products, and popular items from that time.

Create a shopping list of items you think a family might need or want to purchase in 1974.

Try to include a variety of products, from groceries to household items and even some items related to pop culture or trends.

After completing your shopping list, compare it to the suggested items listed in the book.

Sample Shopping List (1974):

Loaf of Wonder Bread

Jell-O dessert mix

Tang instant drink mix (to enjoy with breakfast)

Canned vegetables (like peas and corn)

TV Guide magazine

Vinyl record album (e.g., the latest hit music)

Bell-bottom jeans

A lava lamp (a trendy home decor item)

1974 A Time Traveler's Guide: Flashback Series of Memorial Books 79

Hair curlers and hair spray

A pet rock (a quirky fad from the '70s)

Feel free to add more items to your shopping list based on your knowledge of 1974 and the information from the book. Once you've created your list, you can compare it to the suggested items from the book to see how well you captured the essence of shopping in the 1970s.

	Item	Price	# Units	Total Price
☐				
☐				
☐				
☐				
☐				
☐				
☐				
☐				
☐				
☐				
☐				
☐				
☐				
☐				
☐				
☐				
☐				
☐				
			Total	

SHOPPING *List*

	Item	Price	# Units	Total Price
☐				
☐				
☐				
☐				
☐				
☐				
☐				
☐				
☐				
☐				
☐				
☐				
☐				
☐				
☐				
☐				
☐				
☐				
☐				
☐				
			Total	

Chapter 8
The Famous Wedding and Divorce of 1974

In the annals of history, 1974 will forever be remembered for a wedding that captured the hearts of millions around the world. It was a celebration of love, glamour, and tradition that transcended borders and generations. This chapter delves into the remarkable wedding that etched itself into the pages of history.

8.1 Famous Wedding

1. Faye Dunaway and Peter Wolf:

On August 7, 1974, American actress Faye Dunaway, aged 33 at the time, wed American rock singer Peter Wolf, aged 28, known for his association with the J. Geils Band.

2. Tim Rice and Jane McIntosh:

On August 19, 1974, British lyricist Tim Rice, who later achieved EGOT status (winning Emmy, Grammy, Oscar, and Tony Awards), married British actress Jane McIntosh. Tim Rice was 29 years old at the time.

3. Quincy Jones Jr. and Peggy Lipton:

On September 14, 1974, American composer, arranger, and producer Quincy Jones Jr., aged 41, married American actress Peggy Lipton, aged 28, best known for her role in "Mod Squad." They were wed in Los Angeles, California. However, their marriage ended in divorce in 1990.

4. Liza Minnelli and Jack Haley, Jr.:

On September 15, 1974, American singer and actress Liza Minnelli, aged 27, married American film and documentary director Jack Haley, Jr., aged 40. This was Minnelli's second marriage, and unfortunately, it also ended in divorce in 1979.

5. Sissy Spacek and Jack Fisk:

On April 12, 1974, Sissy Spacek, the actress known for her role in "Coal Miner's Daughter," tied the knot with art director Jack Fisk. This wedding marked a special moment in the life of the talented actress and the art director. Sissy Spacek's portrayal of country music legend Loretta Lynn in "Coal Miner's Daughter" would later earn her acclaim and recognition in the film industry.

8.2 Famous divorces

In 1974, several high-profile divorces among celebrities made headlines:

1. George Foreman and Adrienne Calhoun:

On February 13, 1974, professional boxer George Foreman, aged 25 at the time, divorced Adrienne Calhoun, bringing an end to their almost 3 years of marriage.

2. Cher and Sonny Bono:

On February 20, 1974, American singer and actress Cher, aged 27, filed for separation from her husband, singer-songwriter Sonny Bono, aged 38.

3. Maggie Smith and Robert Stephens:

On May 6, 1974, actress Maggie Smith, aged 39, divorced actor Robert Stephens, aged 42, after 6 years of marriage.

4. Elizabeth Taylor and Richard Burton:

On June 26, 1974, English-American actress Elizabeth Taylor went through her 5th divorce, this time from Welsh actor Richard Burton, after just over 10 years of marriage. Their on-again, off-again relationship was widely publicized.

5. Elizabeth Montgomery and William Asher:

On October 10, 1974, actress Elizabeth Montgomery, aged 41, divorced director-producer William Asher, aged 53, after 11 years of marriage.

These celebrity divorces highlighted the complexities of love and relationships in the world of fame and entertainment, and they often garnered significant media attention during that time.

Activity
Wedding and Divorce Timeline Challenge

In this activity, we'll test your knowledge of the famous weddings and divorces of 1974 from Chapter 8. Your task is to arrange these events in chronological order based on their dates. Can you recall when these significant moments took place?

Instructions:

Read the descriptions of the famous weddings and divorces from 1974.

Arrange these events in chronological order, starting with the earliest date and ending with the latest date.

Write the event number next to the date to indicate the order (e.g., 1, 2, 3, 4, 5).

Once you've arranged them in chronological order, check your answers below.

Events:

- ☐ Faye Dunaway and Peter Wolf's Wedding
- ☐ Sissy Spacek and Jack Fisk's Wedding
- ☐ George Foreman and Adrienne Calhoun's Divorce
- ☐ Tim Rice and Jane McIntosh's Wedding
- ☐ Cher and Sonny Bono's Separation
- ☐ Quincy Jones Jr. and Peggy Lipton's Wedding
- ☐ Liza Minnelli and Jack Haley, Jr.'s Wedding
- ☐ Maggie Smith and Robert Stephens' Divorce
- ☐ Elizabeth Taylor and Richard Burton's Divorce
- ☐ Elizabeth Montgomery and William Asher's Divorce

1974 A Time Traveler's Guide: Flashback Series of Memorial Books 91

Dates:
- ☐ April 12, 1974
- ☐ August 7, 1974
- ☐ August 19, 1974
- ☐ September 14, 1974
- ☐ September 15, 1974
- ☐ February 13, 1974
- ☐ February 20, 1974
- ☐ June 26, 1974
- ☐ October 10, 1974

Now, arrange these events in chronological order based on their dates.

How well do you remember the sequence of these famous weddings and divorces from 1974? Compare your answers to the correct chronological order to find out!

1974 — A Time Traveler's Guide: Flashback Series of Memorial Books — 92

Unleash your creativity and bring the famous 1974 wedding to life with vibrant colors in this exciting coloring wedding picture activity

1974 A Time Traveler's Guide: Flashback Series of Memorial Books 93

1974 A Time Traveler's Guide: Flashback Series of Memorial Books 94

Relaxing Corner
1974 Review Crossword

Instructions:

Solve the crossword by filling in the blanks with the correct words or phrases related to the events and facts of 1974.
Read the book or use your knowledge of the year 1974 to complete the crossword.
Have fun and test your memory!
Crossword Clues:

ACROSS

6. The host nation that won the FIFA World Cup in 1974.
7. American singer and actress who filed for separation from singer-songwriter Sonny Bono in 1974.
8. The iconic sports car of 1974 produced by Lamborghini.
9. The popular subcompact car of 1974 praised for its reliability and low repair costs.

DOWN

1. American actress who wed American rock singer Peter Wolf in 1974.
2. The major sporting event held in New Zealand in 1974 that ended a long winning streak for UCLA in basketball.
3. British lyricist who married British actress Jane McIntosh in August 1974.
4. American actress known for her role in "Coal Miner's Daughter" who wed art director Jack Fisk in 1974.
5. The famous singer and actress who married American film director Jack Haley, Jr. in 1974.

Crossword Puzzle:

Have fun solving the crossword and reviewing the exciting events of 1974!

Special gift for readers
We have heartfelt thank-you gifts for you

As a token of our appreciation for joining us on this historical journey through 1974, we've included a set of cards and stamps inspired by the year of 1974. These cards are your canvas to capture the essence of the past. We encourage you to use them as inspiration for creating your own unique cards, sharing your perspective on the historical moments we've explored in this book. Whether it's a holiday greeting or a simple hello to a loved one, these cards are your way to connect with the history we've uncovered together.

Happy creating!

JOY

Photo goes here

SHARE THE MEMORIES

Merry Christmas

Photos goes here

The . . . .

Let's celebrate this year

Embracing 1974: A Grateful Farewell

Thank you for joining us on this journey through a year that holds a special place in our hearts. Whether you experienced 1974 firsthand or through the pages of this book, we hope it brought you moments of joy, nostalgia, and connection to a time that will forever shine brightly in our memories.

Share Your Thoughts and Help Us Preserve History

Your support and enthusiasm for this journey mean the world to us. We invite you to share your thoughts, leave a review, and keep the spirit of '74 alive. As we conclude our adventure, we look forward to more journeys through the annals of history together. Until then, farewell and thank you for the memories.

We would like to invite you to explore more of our fantastic world by scanning the QR code below. There you can easily get free ebooks from us and receive so many surprises.

Copyright © Edward Art Lab

All rights reserved. No part of this publication may be reproduce distributed, or transmitted in any form or by any means, including photocopying, recording, or other electronic or mechanical methods, without the prior written permission of the publisher, except in the case of brief quotations embodied in critical reviews and certain other noncommercial uses permitted by copyright law.

TO DO LIST

well done!

TO DO LIST

-
-
-
-
-
-
-
-
-
-
-
-
-
-

well done!

To Do List

- [ ] _____
- [ ] _____
- [ ] _____
- [ ] _____
- [ ] _____
- [ ] _____
- [ ] _____
- [ ] _____
- [ ] _____
- [ ] _____
- [ ] _____
- [ ] _____
- [ ] _____
- [ ] _____
- [ ] _____

To Do List

- [ ] _____
- [ ] _____
- [ ] _____
- [ ] _____
- [ ] _____
- [ ] _____
- [ ] _____
- [ ] _____
- [ ] _____
- [ ] _____
- [ ] _____
- [ ] _____
- [ ] _____
- [ ] _____

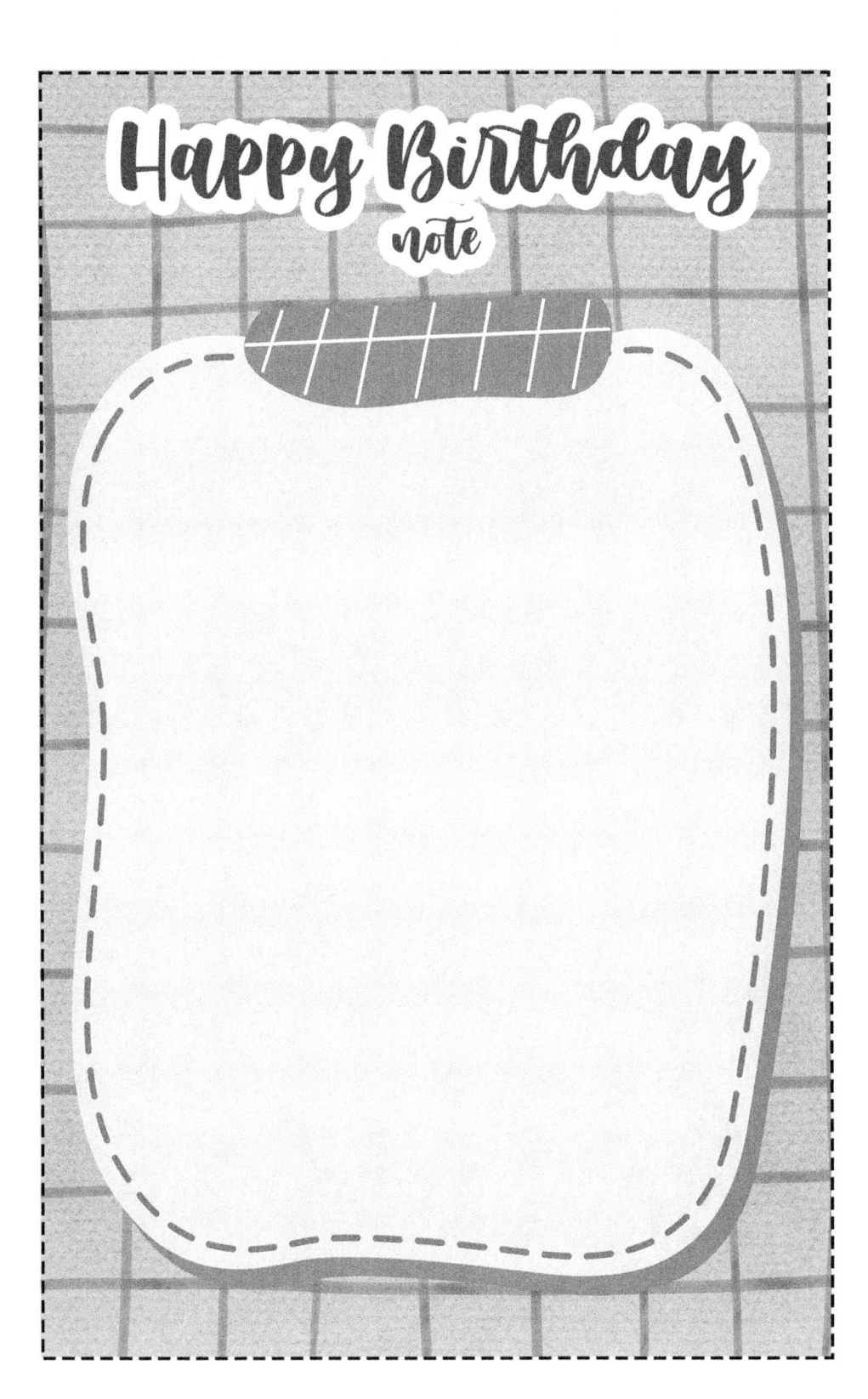

Happy Birthday
note

Happy Birthday
note

Happy Birthday
note

HAPPY BIRTHDAY NOTE

TO DO LIST

Name: _____   Day: _____   Month: _____

No	To Do List	Yes	No

TO DO LIST

Name: _____ Day: _____ Month: _____

No	To Do List	Yes	No

TO DO LIST

Name: _____ Day: _____ Month: _____

No	To Do List	Yes	No

NOTE

Postcard

N
W
E
S
Greetings!
TIME TO
TRAVEL
2
PACIFIC OCEAN
MAP OF
THE WORLD

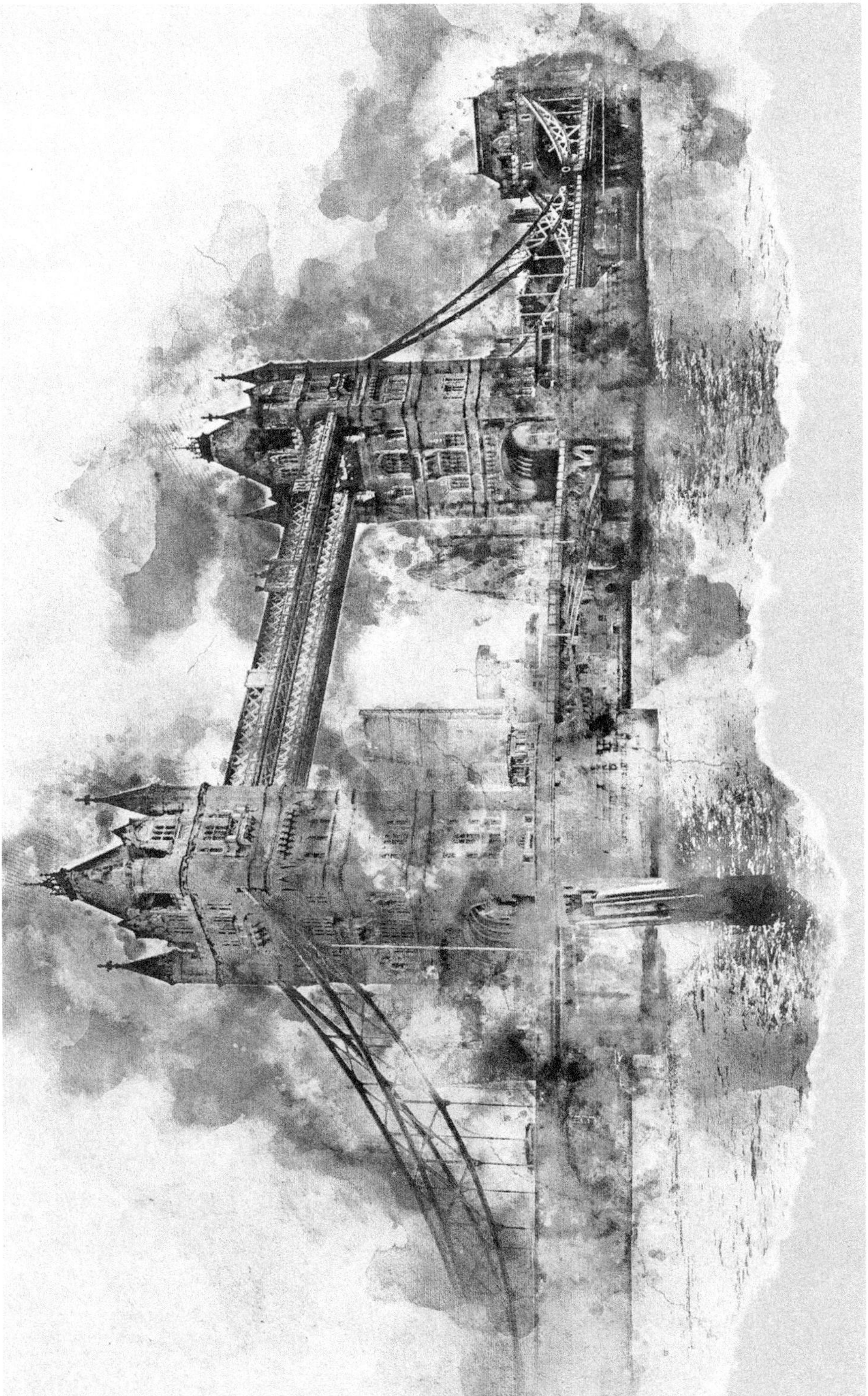

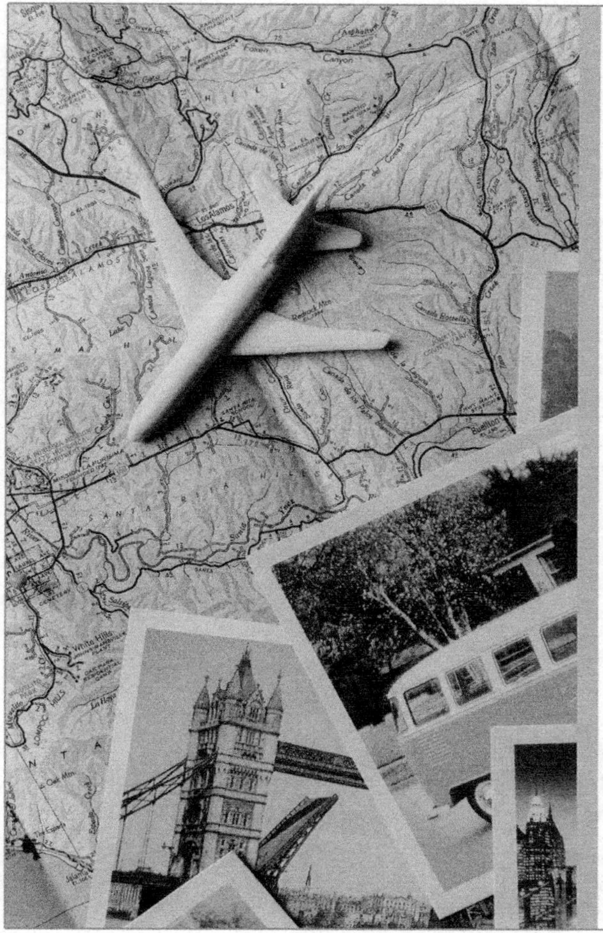

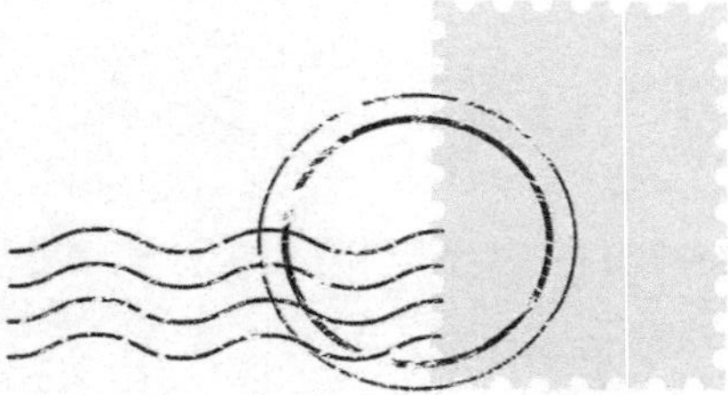

To:

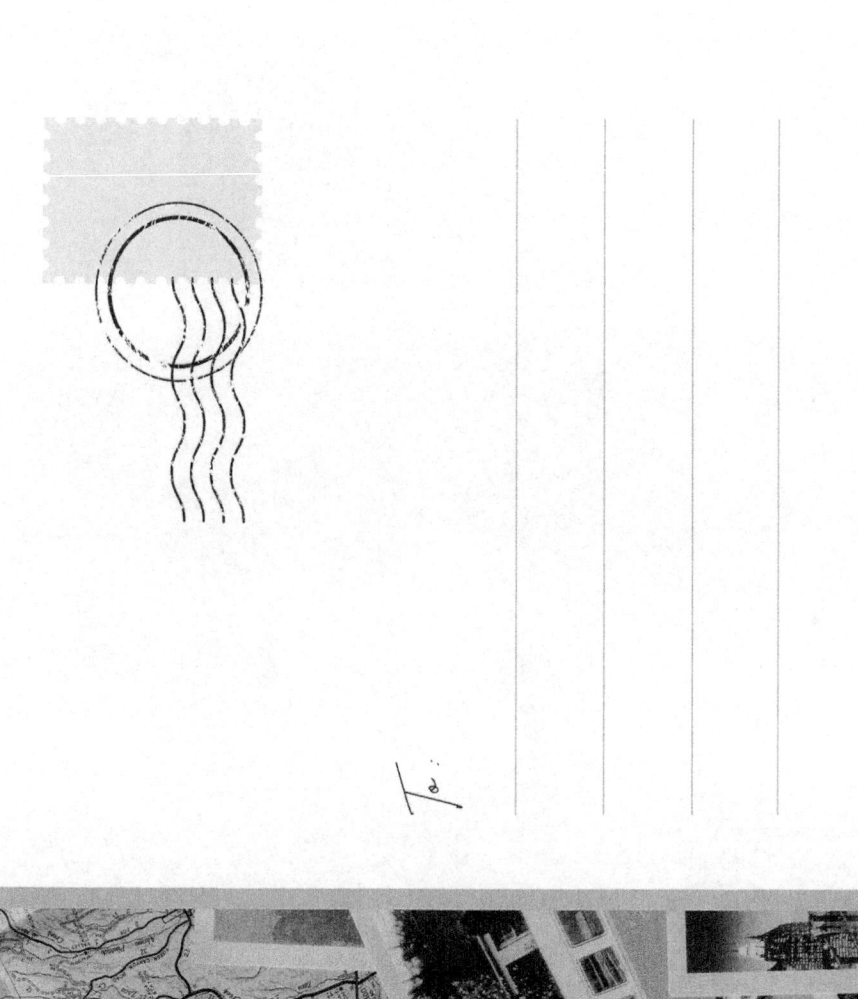

Remember This!

WISH YOU WERE HERE,
123 ANYWHERE ST., ANY CITY

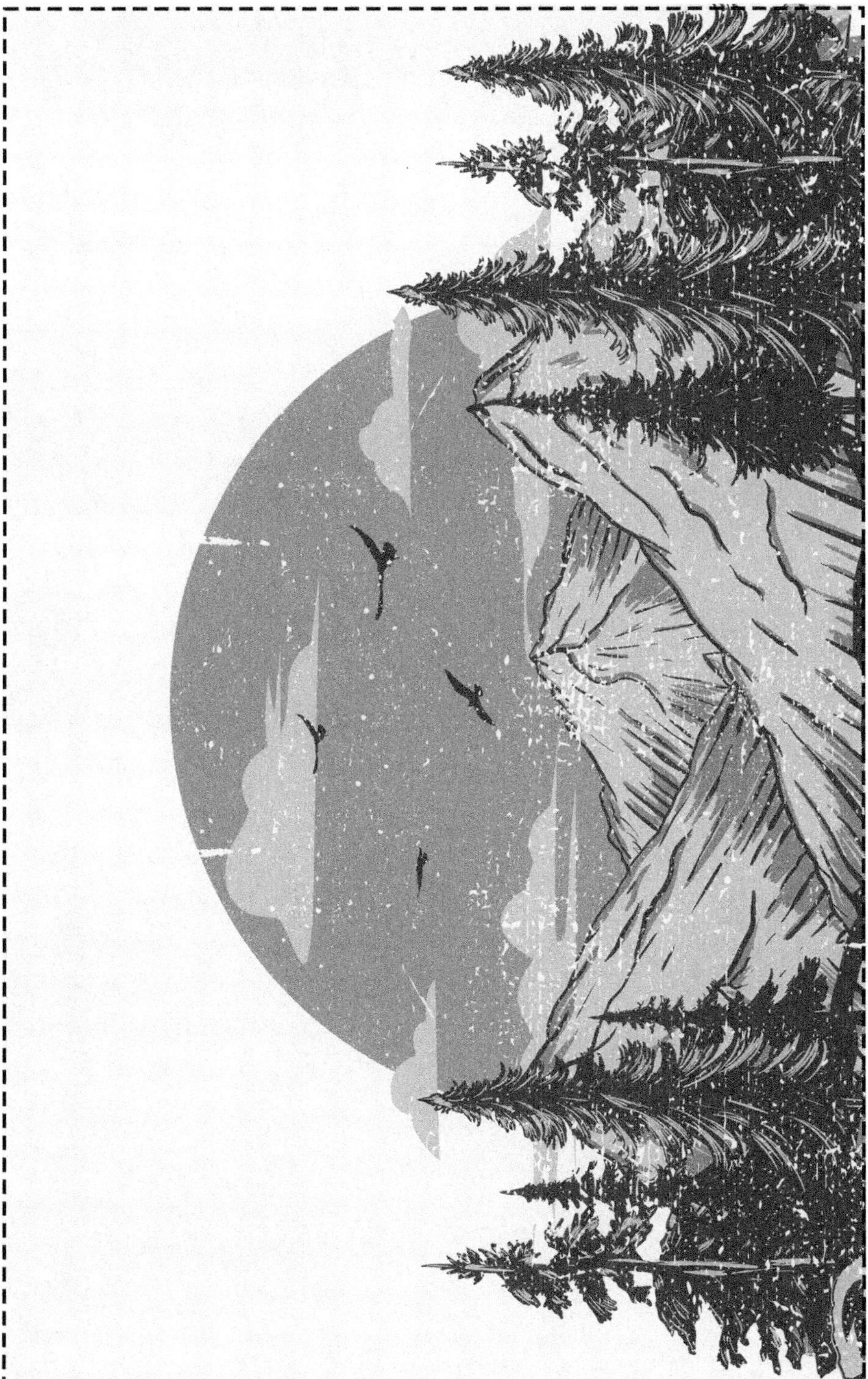

POSTCARD

To:

From:

Printed in Great Britain
by Amazon